"I'll be Your Server"
The Heart of Christian
Discipleship
Profiles in Servanthood

Gordon S. Jackson

M✝ Zion Ridge Press
Books Off the Beaten Path

www.MtZionRidgePress.com

Mt Zion Ridge Press LLC
295 Gum Springs Rd, NW
Georgetown, TN 37366

https://www.mtzionridgepress.com

ISBN 13: 978-1-962862-30-1

Published in the United States of America
Publication Date: October 2024
Copyright: © 2024 Gordon S. Jackson

Editor-In-Chief: Michelle Levigne
Executive Editor: Tamera Lynn Kraft

Cover art design by Tamera Lynn Kraft
Cover Art Copyright by Mt Zion Ridge Press LLC © 2024

"[W]hoever wants to become great among you must be your servant, and whoever wants to be first must be slave of all. For even the Son of Man did not come to be served, but to serve, and to give his life as a ransom for many."

— Mark 10:43-45

"If you wish to be a leader you will be frustrated, for very few people wish to be led. If you aim to be a servant you will never be frustrated."

— Frank F. Warren[1]

---

[1] Quoted in Gordon S. Jackson: *Quotes for the Journey, Wisdom for the Way*, 151

Table of Contents

Introduction

"Hello, my name's Cassie and I'll be your server tonight. Is there anything that I can get you to drink to start with?"

Cassie's twenty-three-word introduction is clear, welcoming and predictable. But she's left a lot unsaid, which, based on our previous visits to restaurants, is assumed. She doesn't need to say that she's there to take care of all our dining needs; we know that. Presumably, she's qualified to answer any questions about the menu. She's also a good listener and notes that I'd like to have mashed potato rather than the fries, and that I want no ice, thank you, in my Diet Coke.

If Cassie is an attentive and patient server, she'll show no irritation as our seven-year-old goes back and forth in his customary indecisiveness before settling on the Megaburger Supreme with fries.

As the person responsible for our dining needs, Cassie is expected to do whatever it takes (within reason) to keep us happy. Her role, though, is that of an intermediary. She doesn't prepare the food; she conveys our requests ("No onion in the salad," "The T-bone medium rare please") to the kitchen, where the chef prepares what we've ordered.

Also, her role as server is limited to the context of ordering our meal, bringing it to our table, and ensuring the food is to our satisfaction. I can't expect her to look after our toddler while we eat; her role does not extend to babysitting. Nor can I order her to wash my car during our meal. Cassie is not my slave.

~~~~~

So what does all this have to do with our faith? Like her, we Christians are servers, or "servants," a less comfortable word. But that's essentially what Cassie is as she lives out her duty to attend to our needs. We may employ a gardener or a cleaner, both of whom perform the duties that a century ago we would have unhesitatingly said were done by servants, if we could afford them.

We Christians differ from Cassie, however, in that we're enlisted in God's service, attending to His needs and wishes as best we can determine them. Of crucial importance then, in my role as a server waiting on God, is listening for His needs and wishes.

There's another major difference between Cassie's responsibilities and the expectations God has of me. When her shift finishes at 10 p.m., she steps out of her role as a server. Christians, by contrast, are always on duty as God's servers. Or, to switch to the word we'll use in this book, God's *servants.*

This is therefore a book for Christians who want to serve Jesus more effectively. Drawing on examples from Scripture, *I'll be Your Server* offers you a set of insights that you can apply to your own Christian walk, as you seek to emulate Jesus' example when He said that He "did not come to be served, but to serve..."

First, though, an important disclaimer. This book is not about servant leadership as it applies to Christians; there are plenty of good books on that topic. Nor will we explore in any detail the four passages in Isaiah concerning "the Suffering Servant." This concept, and the extent to which it applies to Jesus and His sufferings, has provided much food for thought for theologians. We will briefly touch on these two topics in the next Profile.

Rather, the book's emphasis is on people we meet in Scripture, individuals like you and me, who for the most part sought to make God-pleasing decisions as they served Him. We'll explore the circumstances of each of these people and the occasion or occasions for service that they encountered. These thirty-six Profiles plus an Introduction will help us identify specific lessons that will enrich our own roles as God's servants.

~~~~~

The book is divided into five sections. Following this Introduction, Part 1 consists of an exploration of the servant role, both in general and specifically in the Christian context. In addition, this section includes a case study of Jesus washing His disciples' feet, an action that epitomizes and models for us His servant heart.

Part 2 introduces us to the servant nature of seven of Scripture's grandest figures, including such obvious choices as Moses, David, and Mary.

Part 3 includes Profiles on other servants who may not be household names but were at least identified by name in Scripture. They include Gideon's servant Purah, Gehazi the greedy servant of Elisha, and Rhoda, the flustered servant who answers the door when Peter comes knocking but forgets to let him in. One identified individual who is included constitutes an exception: the angel Gabriel. He's not human, although in the three instances that we know of he takes on something like a human appearance, as this angelic servant of the Lord brings important messages from God.

Part 4 looks at some of the numerous servants in Scripture who were seen as incidental players, whose names don't even show up in the credits at the end of the movie.

Finally, Part 5 provides some concluding thoughts on the concept of Christians as servants, pulling together some of the book's main themes.

~~~~~

Why this emphasis on individuals who play a servant role in Scripture, rather than an extended analysis of general aspects of Christian service? It is because we more easily relate to the concrete examples of real-life people than abstract principles. I can identify with a Moses, a Paul, or a Rhoda, or any of the other individuals we'll meet in the pages ahead. I can't as easily relate to an abstract quality of servanthood, like humility. But show me a person and tell me what he or she did, and I can immediately make a connection. I can relate to the fact that perhaps they faced difficulties, were afraid, or simply didn't know where to turn to next. Yes, like them, we know what it means to be in God's service, with the challenges and difficulties that may entail.

Most of us already have a good handle on what it means to be a servant, at least in theory if not in practice, and in general, if not in the specifics. However, by looking at these case studies, we'll go beyond the general and get into the different, concrete circumstances that these biblical servants faced. We will see how they lived out their servant roles in actual, real-life circumstances. They responded to their unique situations with an authenticity that can offer us a close-up look at what it means to be a servant.

~~~~~

Grasping some general principles about a biblical understanding of servanthood is good and well. But under the Holy Spirit's leadership, as you read each of the Bible studies that follow, you may have deeper spiritual insights from these encounters with biblical servants. See these entries, then, as potential triggers for illumination that might not come from a more generic look at biblical servanthood.

For these reasons, we will exclude the numerous instances in Jesus' parables that include servants. Nor will we look at those individuals who identify themselves as the servant of the Lord or as a king's faithful servant. In these uses, the speaker is pointing more to his or her status as a subject of God or a monarch, or some other person of higher status. They are not necessarily identifying with an actual person filling a servant role, as we are exploring it here.

~~~~~

But first, some practical matters. All scripture references are from the *New International Version* of the Bible, except where noted otherwise. Then there is the issue of inclusive language. Some quotes use "man," "mankind" and so on when referring to people in general. These quotes reflect earlier usage which characterizes contemporary English less and less. In keeping with my commitment to present all sources as accurately as possible, I have included these entries with their original wording.[2]

---

[2] The use of masculine pronouns to refer to God is done with due deference to concerns about inclusive language. Their use is not to assert that God is masculine. Where possible, attempts have been made to avoid masculine pronouns. But they have been included rather than resort to the heavy-handed artificiality of writing things like "We seek to know who God is, how God deals with us, and what God

Another usage issue concerns the name for "God" in Old Testament references. I have tried to bear in mind that when "LORD" (all capitals) is used in the *NIV*, it is signifying the Hebrew word "Yahweh." So I have often used that term when the context involves Old Testament characters. But I have not been consistent and have at times treated "God" and "Yahweh" more or less interchangeably.

Then, regarding wording: I use "chapter" to refer to the Scripture readings. To avoid confusion, I will refer to the chapters in this book as "Profiles."

How to use this book? You can dip into it wherever you want, reading the entries in whatever sequence you like. I urge you, however, to do the assigned reading at the beginning of each Profile, especially if it is a passage unfamiliar to you. You may want to use these Profiles for your personal devotions. If you do, consider writing a brief response to each Profile, especially in conjunction with other elements of your devotional time, such as prayer or Bible reading.

These entries may occasionally interpret Scripture differently from your own understanding. If that occurs, feel free to rely on your own understanding of these Bible passages. But please don't let any such differences distract you from an entry's main point.

I hope that the insights that follow will deepen your own faith and help you in one way or another to share the marvelous riches of God's Kingdom with those whose lives you will touch.

---

wants to characterize our life together as God's people." Elsewhere, quoted material using these pronouns is left unchanged, respecting the need to accurately present these sources.

PART 1: SETTING THE STAGE

1: Service, Servants and Servanthood

Former college president Frank Warren said, "If you wish to be a leader you will be frustrated, for very few people wish to be led. If you aim to be a servant, you will never be frustrated."[3] Yet in our society we continue to place a high premium on leadership potential in our young people. Some surveys have yielded amusing results, in which the great majority of college students, especially men, see themselves as "above average" in their leadership ability. (Like the fictional Lake Wobegon, in Garrison Keillor's radio show, *Prairie Home Companion*, where all the children are above average.)

Aspiring leaders will find much food for thought in Scripture. According to the Bible Gateway website, the words "leader" or "leaders" appear 236 times in the *New International Version*. By contrast, the words "servant" or "servants" are mentioned far more often (767 times), giving us at least one rough measure of which group of people merit more attention.

Plenty of biblical characters are, of course, leaders who also fill servant roles, including major figures like Moses, David and Jesus, of whom we know much. Many others, though, play seemingly incidental roles as servants, but only *seemingly* so. For they are all part of God's unfolding plans as revealed in both the Old and New Testaments. Some of these obscure, little known individuals aren't even identified. Think for example of the two servants who accompany Abraham and Isaac most of the way to Mount Moriah, where the patriarch fully expects to sacrifice his long-awaited son to God. Or there's the young Israelite girl who was captured in a Syrian raid on some Israeli village or town and dragooned into service as a maid in the house of Naaman the leper. She too is unidentified.

Notice, as an aside, the difference between someone who is described as *unnamed* versus someone who is *unidentified*, an error we often see in our news media. The people whose names we don't know, like Abraham's two servants, and the young maid, certainly had names. They were not nonentities; humble though their roles were, they were individuals like you and me, greatly beloved of God, and also vitally important in the Bible story. Let us never underestimate the contribution that these players had in God's drama, whether they had a speaking role or not. Servants, in other words, matter — and they matter in the biblical narrative too.

Returning to the Warren quote about aiming to be a servant, ask

---

[3] Quoted in Gordon S. Jackson: *Quotes for the Journey, Wisdom for the Way*, 151

yourself: When did a professor or a pastor last write a letter of recommendation saying, "Mike has great servanthood-potential"? Nobody wants to be a servant, it seems; that's for losers. But that was not how Jesus thought. In His characteristic way He turned societal values upside down. Even His disciples weren't immune to the "aspiring leadership" bug, as when James and John approached Jesus and asked, "Let one of us sit at your right and the other at your left in your glory." (Mk. 10:37)

Jesus wasn't impressed. Instead, as He had *previously* laid down His expectations elsewhere, His followers should be striving for servanthood, not leadership: "Jesus called the Twelve and said, 'Anyone who wants to be first must be the very last, and the servant of all.'" (Mk. 9:35) They still hadn't got the point. And two millennia later many of us haven't either.

Let us turn now to two types of servanthood. One is what we could term general servanthood. The other is Christian servanthood, that which is distinctly biblical: the servant's role as seen from God's perspective.

Servanthood Generally

A good servant is characterized, at a minimum, by these six qualities. None of them is surprising. Yet it is worth spelling them out as a foundation for the kind of servants that Christians ought to be.

Attentiveness: We all hate being ignored or left to ourselves when we want help. If we've been seated at a restaurant and have waited, say, fifteen minutes for someone to bring us menus, we won't be impressed. Or if the food takes an unduly long time to make it to our table. Similarly, if we're on the phone to our credit card company and are put on hold, and made to wait and wait and wait, we'll think little of their service. Quite how we define a "reasonable time" before being attended to will vary from one setting to another. It will also vary from one person to another, depending on our threshold of patience. The principle remains, though: we expect someone responsible for waiting on us to do so reasonably promptly.

Cheerfulness: We expect people who are serving us to convey a suitably pleasant demeanor, either actual cheerfulness if that's appropriate or at least a positive attitude. Sticking with the restaurant example, we expect to be greeted with a smile from the person who seats us at our table. We'd expect a comparably warm greeting when checking into a hotel. In a more solemn setting — visiting a funeral home to make arrangements for the service of a loved one, for instance — we'd still expect the person dealing with us to be positive.

Consistency and Reliability: While these could be described separately, for practical purposes they are the same when it comes to service. I want my McDonald's Big Mac to be predictably the same, whether I'm in Alaska or Wyoming. I want a high level of reliability when I order a product from Amazon, that it will be here on (or at least close to) the promised delivery date. Likewise, I expect a consistent level of good service at a Hampton Inn or any other more up-scale hotel.

Empathy: The good servant gets to know me, my interests, and my needs. In our favorite coffee shop, if we are repeat customers we are impressed when a server says, "Good morning, sir; are you once again going to have your decaf latte?" If we were at the funeral home, we'd expect the funeral director to be ultra-sensitive to our loss. Or, by contrast, if I'm in a jewelry store, where my fiancée and I are picking out an engagement ring, we'd expect the clerk to empathize with our joy and not dampen our excitement with a funereal gloominess. In brief, those who seek to serve us well will read us, our mood, and our need.

Knowledge: If I am ordering a meal in a restaurant, I expect the server to know about the items on the menu. If my party is interested in ordering wine, I expect the person to make informed suggestions about what wine would go with which dish. Or imagine a visit to a Lowe's or Home Depot hardware store, where I'm looking for a reticulated inverse shuttle-flanging grommet.[4] I expect a passing staff member either to steer me in the right direction, or else call someone who can help. I don't expect a store associate, who is acting as my servant in this context, to know every product in the store. But I do expect the staff to show they care (some empathy, remember?) and ensure that my question is answered. Related to knowledge is competence: We don't want the server spilling wine on our clothes, getting our order wrong, or getting muddled over the ingredients in the day's special.

Sacrifice: The best service embodies the notion that while the customer may not always be right, the customer is always the customer. We'll do what we can to keep the customer happy, even if it costs us. The story is told of a teen working in a supermarket. He'd been there for only a few weeks and was on duty at the customer service counter when a customer said she might have lost a valuable item in the store. Had it been handed in? He checked, and it hadn't. But noticing how disappointed she was, he gave her a gift certificate for $60, and said, "I'm sorry I couldn't find it but maybe this will make you feel better." Now, he needn't have given her anything at all, let alone a $60 store voucher. But the point was, in his short time working in the store he had learned its culture: You never let a customer leave unhappy or dissatisfied if you can help it.

Similarly, if something goes wrong with our order in the restaurant, or we've had to wait an extraordinarily long time for our food, a shrewd server will either give us a complimentary dessert or in more serious situations, "comp" the entire meal.

~~~~~

Attention to each of these six factors combines to give us excellent

---

[4] I just made that up.

service, produced by skilled and committed servers or others filling the servant role. Thomas Connellan and Ron Zemke, in their book *Sustaining Knock Your Socks Off Service*, say that "Sustaining high quality service is not simply doing well whatever it is you do; it is understanding what is important to the customer and doing *those* things well."[5]

We all have grumbles or even horror stories about service that didn't go right, of airlines that misplaced our checked luggage or the hotel that canceled our reservation because of construction and forgot to tell us. Worse still, in each case the person with whom we dealt regarding the shoddy service seemed not to care. Like the time we sent back the steak that was overdone, and the server glared at us as if it were our fault. Connellan and Zemke would not have approved.

Christian Servanthood

In the business and nonprofit world, providing good service is indispensable. But what happens when we layer on top of the need for trained and committed servers or servants the added expectations we have of Christian servers or servants? We can identify seven considerations that make Christian service distinctive.

Jesus' Teaching, Example and Expectations: We can do no better than look at Jesus' example of servanthood and His expectations of us. In brief, everything about our servant role as Christians arises from our relationship with Him. The heart of His ministry is stated plainly in Matthew's gospel. Right after telling the disciples that if they want to be first, they need to be last, He adds: "… the Son of Man did not come to be served, but to serve, and to give his life as a ransom for many." (Mt. 20:28)

His ultimate act of servanthood was of course His sacrificial death on the cross. But throughout His life He modeled what authentic servanthood looked like. He was attentive to people's needs. He empathized with them. He brought them joy, as He ushered in a new Kingdom that enabled people to discover God's will in their lives in an unprecedented way. It is no coincidence that Albert Schweitzer said, "Every person I have known who has been truly happy, has learned how to serve others."[6]

Motivation: Unlike others who engage in acts of service, the Christian's motivation is unique. It is to please God and in whatever way possible to advance His Kingdom. For Christians, a "God-orientation" is central to who we are and how we live. As Paul said in speaking to the Athenians, "For in him we live and move and have our being." (Acts 17:28)[7]

---

[5] Thomas Connellan and Ron Zemke, *Sustaining Knock Your Socks off Service*, 62.
[6] https://quotefancy.com/quote/764539/Albert-Schweitzer-Every-person-I-have-known-who-has-been-truly-happy-has-learned-how-to. Accessed Sept. 5, 2023.
[7] He was quoting a Cretan philosopher, Epimenides.

As we live out our lives, we ought always to be motivated by the fact that we are in God's service, which demands of us only our best. As Maltbie Babcock said, "[W]oe be to us if we are content with small service... Let us not be easily content... Our King deserves and expects kingliness."[8]

Godly Humility: Jesus' humility overlayed everything He did. Here we have the very Son of God lowering Himself to take on human form. He "emptied" Himself, as Paul writes in a memorable passage in Philippians, when he says of Jesus: "Who, being in very nature God, did not consider equality with God something to be used to his own advantage; rather, he made himself nothing by taking the very nature of a servant, being made in human likeness." (Phil. 2:6-7) What greater model of servant leadership could we ask for? (Jesus' example of foot washing is explored in the next Profile.) Our service ought likewise to be characterized by a godly humility.

Unaware Servanthood: In Matthew 25:37-40 we read Jesus' words:

Then the righteous will answer him, "Lord, when did we see you hungry and feed you, or thirsty and give you something to drink? When did we see you a stranger and invite you in, or needing clothes and clothe you? When did we see you sick or in prison and go to visit you?" The King will reply, "Truly I tell you, whatever you did for one of the least of these brothers and sisters of mine, you did for me."

Here we have Jesus' expectation of servanthood that comes so naturally to us as we see people in need that we don't have to think about it. When His disciples see someone in need, they spring into action.

Paradoxical Servanthood: "Jesus called the Twelve and said, 'Anyone who wants to be first must be the very last, and the servant of all.'" (Mk. 9:35)

We should not be surprised at the upside down, topsy turvy nature of God's world. Tony Campolo wrote a book based on the idea of someone sneaking into a large department store and mischievously mixing up the price tags on everything.[9] A large screen TV would be priced at $9.99, for example, or an ordinary bath towel's new price was an absurd $1,800. Campolo's point is that this is what God's economy is like: The things God values may not be what we value, and vice versa. As Isaiah says, "'For my thoughts are not your thoughts, neither are your ways my ways,' declares the Lord. 'As the heavens are higher than the earth, so are my ways higher than your ways and my thoughts than your thoughts.'" (Is. 55:8-9)

Then there are the beatitudes. How can those who mourn be expected to be happy, for example? Or how can the meek expect to inherit the earth? Yet these upside-down values should come as no surprise to those of us who line up for service in God's Kingdom and are sent to the back of the

---

[8] Maltbie Babcock: *Thoughts for Every-Day Living*, 26.
[9] Tony Campolo: *Who Switched the Price Tags?*

line to be the "very last."

Wholehearted Servanthood: Jesus makes it plain that we either serve Him wholeheartedly, or not at all. The blunt warning to the church in Laodicea leaves us in no doubt about God's expectations of us: "I know your deeds, that you are neither cold nor hot. I wish you were either one or the other!" (Rev. 3:15) Similarly, Jesus Himself tells us that "No one can serve two masters. Either you will hate the one and love the other, or you will be devoted to the one and despise the other." (Mt. 6:24) He points to the tension between seeking to serve God and money, but it could be anything that comes in the way of our commitment to God.

Similarly, James refers to the problem of having divided loyalties, when he says, "such a person is double-minded and unstable in all they do." (Jas. 1:8) Like the *New International Version*, most translations render the word as "double-minded," which is especially interesting in the Greek. It is *dipsuchos*, or "two-souled." That is, the very core of one's being is divided. How can such a being have a wholehearted commitment to anything or anyone?

"Transcending" Servanthood: Strangely, in Jesus' eyes we shift from being servants to the remarkable status of being His friends, as John's gospel notes: "You are my friends if you do what I command. I no longer call you servants, because a servant does not know his master's business. Instead, I have called you friends, for everything that I learned from my Father I have made known to you." (Jn. 15:14-15) He is pointing to the difference in the relationship He has with those who follow Him: slaves obey their master because they have no choice, servants less so perhaps. But friends do things based on a relationship of love.

William Barclay notes that there was no shame in calling oneself "God's slave." Among those who did so were Moses, Joshua, and David. In the New Testament Paul and James described themselves as "slaves of God." Barclay adds, "The greatest men in the past had been proud to be called the *douloi*, the slaves of God. And Jesus says: 'I have something greater for you yet, you are no longer slaves; you are *friends*.' Christ offers an intimacy with God which not even the greatest men knew before He came into the world."[10] Elsewhere in the New Testament we have Paul, James and Jude opening their epistles proudly asserting their status as slaves of Jesus, although the *New International Version* translates each instance as "servant." (Rom. 1:1, James 1:1 and Jude verse 1)

Just as loving couples do things for each other out of love, Christians serve their Lord not because they are required to but because they want to. Think of the relationships in the parable of the prodigal son. By the end of the story, the younger, wayward son has been restored to his loving father, a development that we assume has reignited their loving relationship. The

---

[10] William Barclay: *The Daily Study Bible: The Gospel of John*, vol. 2, 178.

older brother, however, appears to remain caught up in a transactional, duty-bound relationship with the father, one devoid of the love that the father has toward him.

Instead of serving God out of duty (or even worse, out of fear), we are to do so out of joy, seeking to honor Him in all we do. As Paul writes to the Colossians, "[W]hatever you do, whether in word or deed, do it all in the name of the Lord Jesus, giving thanks to God the Father through him." (Col. 3:17)

Oswald Chambers imagined Jesus saying, "I reckon on you for extreme service, with no complaining on your part, and no explanation on mine."[11] Yes, service in the cause of Christ is all-demanding, all-consuming. Yet servanthood comes with inestimable blessings.

We need to be careful here. Our motivation for serving Jesus is to respond to His love with our own; we serve Him out of gratitude, *not* for what we can get out of that relationship. We are not engaged in some kind of business transaction with our Savior. Nevertheless, just as we are blessed in various ways through other loving relationships, so too will our relationship with Jesus bring us blessings. Jesus Himself makes this plain in the parable best known as the story of the talents, or the gold bars (*New International Version*). Those who use the gifts they've been given in their master's service are in turn honored with the words, "Well done, good and faithful servant! You have been faithful with a few things; I will put you in charge of many things. Come and share your master's happiness!" (Mt. 25:21).

The prayer of St. Ignatius speaks to the need to serve with pure motives: "Teach us, good Lord, to serve you as you deserve; to give, and not to count the cost, to fight, and not to heed the wounds, to toil, and not to seek for rest, to labor, and not to ask for reward, except that of knowing that we are doing your will."[12]

~~~~~

A brief word is in order regarding several important passages in Isaiah, which speak about the Suffering Servant.[13] There has been much speculation on who is being referred to in the four Isaiah passages.[14] However these verses are understood in their Old Testament context, Christians see a dual meaning, which includes identification of Jesus with

---

[11] Oswald Chambers: *My Utmost for His Highest*, Dec. 18.

[12] Quoted in *Doubleday Prayer Collection*, **88**.

[13] The passages are Isaiah 42:1-4; 49:1-6; 50:4-11,; and 52:13-53:12.

[14] Some scholars see a split between a collective servant, the nation of Israel (when it is obeying God's will), or an individual servant, possibly the Messiah. But other leaders have been suggested too, such as Cyrus, the relatively enlightened Persian king who looked favorably on the Israelites, thereby acting as an unwitting servant for God.

this material. This is because of the numerous and explicit references to these Old Testament passages, in which Jesus can accurately be described as the servant of Yahweh. This servant undergoes suffering in His Father's name. The *Eerdman's Bible Dictionary* identifies some of these parallels:

> When Jesus predicts his suffering and death (Mk. 9:12, 31; 10:33; Luke 23:7) he is probably reflecting on the Servant Songs. In more specific parallels, Jesus came to serve and to give his life a ransom for many (Mt. 20:28…Is. 53:11-12); he was silent before his accusers (Mt. 26:63… Is. 53:7); and interceded for sinners on the cross (Luke 23:34, Is. 53:12).

Much more could be said on this topic. But for our purposes it is sufficient to underscore what the church has long recognized: Jesus underwent unimaginable suffering on our behalf, in His role as God's servant. Paul brings the suffering and servanthood themes together in his letter to the Philippians, when he writes, "And being found in appearance as a man, he humbled himself by becoming obedient to death—even death on a cross!" (Phil. 2:8) What more need we say about Jesus as the Suffering Servant?

~~~~~

Finally, we need to say a word about servant leadership, a notion popularized in a 1970 essay by Robert Greenleaf, titled *The Servant as Leader*. Subsequently developed into a book, it became a classic for managers and other leaders. Scores of books on this theme have appeared in the last half century, as well as several academic journals reporting research on the concept. Greenleaf established a Center for Servant Leadership, which notes that:

> A servant-leader focuses primarily on the growth and well-being of people and the communities to which they belong. While traditional leadership generally involves the accumulation and exercise of power by one at the "top of the pyramid," servant leadership is different. The servant-leader shares power, puts the needs of others first and helps people develop and perform as highly as possible.[15]

~~~~~

The concept has resonated well with Christian readers because of its compatibility with Jesus' emphasis on selflessness and putting others first. This book's focus is on individual servants in Scripture and the lessons we can learn from them. In many of these instances, especially the Profile on Jesus, we see examples of servant leadership that long predated Greenleaf's formulation of the idea. We'll leave it to you to decide which of the people we'll examine meet Greenleaf's definition.

~~~~~

---

[15] https://www.greenleaf.org/what-is-servant-leadership/. Accessed April 16, 2024.

Now it is time to examine biblical servanthood in action. We will explore thirty-five case studies. First, we will look at Jesus' example as He washes His disciples' feet, an action that captures the essence of His ministry and example as a servant. Then we will look at two categories of servants: those who are more prominent or better known, and those who, while more obscure, nevertheless also played their part in advancing God's Kingdom, whether they knew it or not.

Regardless of their prominence in Scripture, what we can learn from all those who sought to act in God's service—even those in the Old Testament—is to honor what the *New Zealand Prayer Book* describes as the purpose of ministry: "It is to continue Jesus' servant ministry in the world by witnessing to God's reconciling love, to bring in the Kingdom of God, to build up the body of Christ, and to glorify God's holy name."[16] And mirroring His servant ministry itself.

---

[16] *The New Zealand Prayerbook*, 932.

2: The Jesus Who Serves — A Case Study

Read John 13:2-16

Key Verses: *"… so he got up from the meal, took off his outer clothing, and wrapped a towel around his waist. After that, he poured water into a basin and began to wash his disciples' feet, drying them with the towel that was wrapped around him." (Verses 4-5)*

~~~~~

"Few incidents in the gospel story [of the foot washing] so reveal the character of Jesus and so perfectly show his love."

— William Barclay[17]

~~~~~

Adriaan Vlok was the minister of law and order in the notorious apartheid government in South Africa, which for more than four decades implemented its policy of racial separation. As part of his duties during the last years of apartheid, he oversaw widespread brutality, including murders, toward those opposing the government.

One of those opponents was the Rev. Frank Chikane, then head of the South African Council of Churches, an organization that was a long-time critic of the government. In 1989 Vlok authorized Chikane's poisoning in an attempted murder, but he survived. Vlok also authorized the bombing of the SACC's headquarters in Johannesburg, among other attacks on organizations and individuals opposing the white government.

But after the fall of apartheid, Vlok had what he described as a born-again Christian experience. Feeling compelled to repent of his various criminal acts he went before the country's Truth and Reconciliation Commission to apply for amnesty. He was the only apartheid government minister to do so.

Vlok subsequently confessed publicly to even more wrongdoing. He engaged in various charitable activities in black communities to atone for his actions, including starting a child feeding program. But his most dramatic act of penance came when he approached Chikane and asked forgiveness for the poison attack. He visited the SACC leader in his office and washed the feet of the man whose death he had previously ordered. He did the same for a group of ten black women whose teenage sons were killed by the police.

It is difficult to imagine a more powerful symbol of a man seeking

---

[17] William Barclay: *The Daily Study Bible: The Gospel of John*, vol. 2, 137.

forgiveness who, following Jesus' example, engages in this act of humility toward those whom he has profoundly hurt.

Some South Africans viewed Vlok's actions skeptically, saying they were too little, too late. How, some people asked, could a man who had overseen such evil actions be forgiven? Yet anyone who met him couldn't help being convinced that his Christian faith and repentance were genuine.[18] His acts of foot washing vividly demonstrated the humility, and authentic repentance, that characterized the genuine Christian faith he came to only late in life. He died in January 2023.

~~~~~

By contrast, Jesus' entire life was a ministry of service; His was not a late-in-life faith. Nor was it necessary for Him to repent of any wrongdoing, let alone the kind of grievous sins of which Adriaan Vlok was guilty. Jesus honored His Father by accomplishing His will, but also by serving us in the ultimate way: by dying on the cross so that we should "not perish but have everlasting life." (Jn. 3:16) An entire book could be written on the servanthood that permeated everything that Jesus did. We will instead focus on just one incident in His life, during His final meal with His disciples. In an act of utter humility He washes their feet, including those of Peter, who characteristically at first refuses to let Jesus serve him in that way.

What are we to make of Jesus' action? Why did He do this, and what lessons does this episode hold for His disciples today? Let's break this down into four parts: The context; the foot washing itself; Peter's response; and Jesus' admonition to the disciples.

The Context: We turn to Luke's gospel for an unhappy aspect of the Last Supper. While sharing this meal with their Lord, "A dispute also arose among them as to which of them was considered to be greatest." (Lk. 22:24) Here, during the most solemn hour as Jesus is increasingly focused on His impending death, and during this farewell dinner, the disciples bicker over which of them is top dog. Have they learned nothing about servanthood and humility in their three years with Jesus? Apparently not.

Imagine having an extended family dinner to honor Grandpa's ninetieth birthday, made all the more poignant because we all know he has stage 4 cancer and won't live to be ninety-one. Then, cousin Ed and grandson Tom start arguing over who should inherit Grandpa's valuable antique coin collection. Aunt Rita and granddaughter Milly are in the corner, trying to outmaneuver brother Rod over the future use of Grandpa's lake cabin...

Yet there is an added dimension in the upper room that night: the Judas factor. Jesus knew that this disciple, whom He had chosen and whom He

---

[18] I met him in January 2016, when he spoke to a group of students whom I was leading on a study program in South Africa.

loved no less than the other eleven, was about to do the unthinkable. As Luke puts it, Jesus says "the hand of him who is going to betray me is with mine on the table." (Lk. 22:21) This led to more conversation among them as they wondered who the betrayer would be, thus heightening the divisiveness and tension among them.

Finally, Jesus was all too aware of what lay ahead. This Profile's assigned reading said, "Jesus knew that the Father had put all things under his power, and that he had come from God and was returning to God..." (verse 3) He was acutely aware of His divine status and origin. Yet shortly He would voluntarily have His humanity crushed out of Him, something which He as God could have avoided with a divine snap of the fingers. As we know from His time in Gethsemane, however, He agonizingly continued to comply with His Father's will, well aware that death awaited Him soon. Yes, He would see the disciples again after His resurrection. But His pre-crucifixion ministry was now wrapping up and "Jesus knew that the hour had come for him to leave this world and go to the Father." (Jn. 13:13)

This was the most solemn of moments. Yet it was marked by dissension among His followers, imminent betrayal by a beloved disciple, and the looming awareness that death and the ordeal leading up to it far overshadow the heartache Grandpa felt in the family gathering that evening. Yet notwithstanding these pressures and potential distractions, Jesus stayed focused on His servant role of heading toward the cross.

The Foot Washing Itself: Many commentators note how the act of washing the feet of one's guests upon entering one's home was an expected courtesy, especially after a long journey. The most menial of tasks was undertaken by the most menial of servants, typically a slave. If no slave were available some other servant would perform this duty.

Jesus pointedly spoke to this duty when He entered the house of Simon the Pharisee, who neglected to provide water to wash Jesus' feet. Moreover, Simon in his thoughts hypocritically condemned the woman who washed Jesus' feet with her tears, dried them with her hair, and anointed them with expensive perfume. Jesus then highlighted both Simon's lack of hospitality and judgmentalism. (Lk. 7:36-50)

In the Last Supper, though, things are turned upside down and the Master washed the feet of those who should serve. None of the disciples had thought to undertake this humble chore. Or if they had, they put the thought out of their minds and left it to someone else. That's where Jesus stepped in, removing His outer clothing and wrapping a towel around His waist. In doing so, Jesus now took on the appearance of a slave. And in doing the actual washing, He performed the duties of a slave as well.

It was as if Jesus had come to your house to stay and you hadn't bothered to prepare for His arrival. So He ends up doing your duties as a host. He washes the dishes, puts fresh linens on the bed, and—most embarrassing to you—He gets down on His knees and cleans a toilet that needs serious attention. This analogy is not to imply that Jesus would seek to embarrass you as His host; rather, it is to suggest the kind of humbling to which He would reduce Himself on your behalf, as He did at the Last Supper.

Peter's Response: Peter now asserted that Jesus should not be washing his feet. Perhaps he was ashamed because he hadn't taken on the task of washing his fellow disciples and Jesus Himself. Perhaps too, the disciples normally took turns as the designated foot washer, and it wasn't his turn today. But for Jesus Himself to take on this task was totally inappropriate, Peter thought. The master should not wash His followers' feet. Jesus had it all backwards, and he told Jesus so.

Then came Jesus' rejoinder: "Unless I wash you, you have no part with me." (Verse 8) Jesus' words now took on profound symbolic meaning. Looking back, we see in the Old Testament that foot washing was part of the ritual for cleaning the priests. Aaron and his sons got specific directions about cleaning their feet and hands before entering God's presence. Being unclean would lead to their death. (Ex. 30:19-21)

Looking forward, we see how foot washing symbolizes at least two things. One is the cleansing of souls that Jesus' death will make possible; the other is the act of baptism that soon became an important rite for Jesus' followers.

Jesus' Admonition to the Disciples: It is no surprise then that Jesus instructed those whose feet He had washed to do the same for each other: "Now that I, your Lord and teacher, have washed your feet, you also should wash one another's feet. I have set you an example that you should do as I have done for you." (Verses 14-15)

This has been taken literally by some Christians, many of whom incorporate foot washing into Maundy Thursday services, mirroring the night of the Last Supper and His betrayal. Others have taken it figuratively, as a powerful picture of Jesus' humility that we should copy however we can. Yet others have taken it theologically, linking it to the aspects of salvation and baptism mentioned above.

Yet whatever insights we glean from exploring this episode in Jesus' life, central to them all is the example of His dual commitment: First, serving His Father by doing His will, by "emptying Himself" and becoming human and, second, by serving humankind to make possible the atonement for our sins.

Which brings us back to Adriaan Vlok's long list of sins and his need for atonement. Beyond the public confession and apologies he made, like Jesus he engaged in these powerful acts of humbling himself.

Jesus, as we have noted, had no need to atone for any sins or wrongs He had done to anyone. Yet Jesus turned upside down the cultural expectations of His day, with the Master becoming the servant. So too with

Adriaan Vlok, once a ruthless cabinet minister, who sought forgiveness from those he had wronged, and modeled Jesus by going on his knees, saying, "I am now your servant."

PART 2: THE SERVANTS WE KNOW WELL

3: David, Following Goliath — The Patient Servant

Read 1 Samuel 17

Key Verse: *"'Whose son are you, young man?' Saul asked him. David said, 'I am the son of your servant Jesse of Bethlehem.'" (Verse 58)*

In his exhilarating account of David and Goliath, the storyteller weaves together two strands. One emphasizes David's reliance on God in his astonishing showdown with the Philistine champion. The other strand is that of David being prepared to take over the monarchy from Saul, something that won't happen for several years yet.

As you read this Profile, remember that previously Samuel had anointed David in anticipation of him serving God as Israel's future monarch. Yet of particular interest here is how, despite his sudden elevation to hero status, David makes no moves to precipitate his ascent to the throne. Knowing he is still young, he is content to bide his time until God sees fit to bring him to power. He bides his time despite astonishing pressure to replace an increasingly erratic and paranoid king. Think of the instance where Saul goes into a cave to relieve himself, the place where David and his men are hiding. Rather than take a perfect opportunity to assassinate his king, David goes out of his way to show Saul that he intends him no harm. (1 Sam. 24)

Beginning with David's encounter with Goliath, then, we see how David isn't the least bit pushy to claim that for which he has been anointed, that which is his destiny. David was a young man of many strengths, and his patience in letting God shape his future undoubtedly belongs on his resume.

The *Africa Bible Commentary* says of 1 Samuel 17, "It is a good principle for us to wait for God to open doors to a ministry for us, rather than trying to force them open ourselves."[19] As you look to your future, remember this lesson from David and his approach to serving God: Don't go looking for Goliaths or other opportunities to serve the Lord, but know that God will in His time both provide you with the challenges and empower you to overcome them.

---

[19] *Africa Bible Commentary*, 355.

4: Gabriel — The Angelic Servant

Read Luke 1:26-38

Key Verse: *"The angel [Gabriel] went to her and said, 'Greetings, you who are highly favored! The Lord is with you.'"* (Verse 28)

Gabriel shows up every year, sort of, in thousands of Christmas pageants around the world, typically with makeshift wings and possibly other shiny accoutrements designed to give him a dazzling appearance. These stand-in Gabriels then repeat some version of the angel's original announcement to young Mary, the exact wording depending on which version of the Bible the pageant director prefers.

But some version of the angel's words echo down the ages, so important was the message entrusted to him as God's servant. Surprisingly, given the importance of his part in preparing Mary for her role as the mother of the Christ-child, Gabriel shows up only four times in the Bible. These include two brief appearances in the Old Testament, in the book of Daniel. His task there is to help Daniel interpret a vision of a ram and a goat. (Dan. 8:15-26 and 9:21-27)

Gabriel's fourth appearance also occurs in Luke 1. He appears before Zechariah to tell him that his apparently barren wife will conceive and bear a son, whom we know will grow up to be John the Baptist.

Gabriel may have appeared elsewhere in Scripture without being identified. However, those four mentions are all we can go on as we try to understand this servant, the one non-human or supra-human character we meet in this book. Nevertheless, even this limited information allows us to note the following about this servant of the Lord.

His Status: We learn in his comment to Zechariah, who is skeptical about the message Gabriel brings him, that: "I am Gabriel. I stand in the presence of God, and I have been sent to speak to you and to tell you this good news." (Lk. 1:19) Notice two things. First, Gabriel's status: he stands in the presence of God Himself. He is no low-level minion in the heavenly hierarchy. Although he isn't described as such in Scripture, Catholic and Orthodox tradition accord him the status of "Archangel," based on the Apocryphal book of Tobit. That's also the title given to Michael, the only other angel who is named in Scripture. (Jude verse 9)

Second, notice the wording, "I have been sent." We need have no doubts about who did the sending. He is an emissary of God Himself. Gabriel is a servant of the highest order, acting on the highest authority. We too serve the "highest authority," a role we should approach with awe.

His Appearance Scares People: In each of the three instances where he interacts with people, we see their fear or awe. Daniel falls on his face: "I was terrified and fell prostrate." (Dan. 8:17) Likewise with Zechariah: "When Zechariah saw him, he was startled and was gripped with fear." (Lk. 1:12) Gabriel tells him not to be afraid, the same assurance he gives Mary, as we see later in the chapter: "Do not be afraid, Mary; you have found favor with God." (Lk. 1:30)

We can only begin to imagine his appearance. We can be sure, though, that it immediately led to a holy, reverential fear. Given his exceptional appearance, he doesn't seem like any ordinary man. Neither the book of Daniel nor Luke's account of Gabriel's appearances give us any more information about him. All we can conclude is that his appearance was frighteningly good.

His "In-Between" Nature: As an angel, Gabriel is in a category of his own as God's servant. He is neither human nor divine. He is able to appear in human form, as a man, as Daniel describes him during Gabriel's second appearance. (Dan. 9:21) But we know nothing about him when he is serving God in a non-earthly way. What does he do when he's standing in the presence of God? Is he waiting for instructions? Being a heavenly being means he transcends time as we know it, so waiting means nothing to him.

Does Gabriel have some kind of post-Easter body, like Jesus' after His resurrection? Is he intervening in the lives of humans in ways that we know nothing about? Nor can we know what kind of divine agenda he is helping to fulfill. Yet we can be confident that unlike the fallen angel, Lucifer, Gabriel is on call for whatever heaven's equivalent of 24/7 is to serve God's bidding.

5: Isaiah — The Vulnerable Servant

Read Isaiah 6:1-8

Key Verse: *"Then I heard the voice of the Lord saying, 'Whom shall I send? And who will go for us?' And I said, 'Here am I. Send me!'"* (Verse 8)

In this awe-inspiring account of Isaiah's call, we encounter something different in the way God intrudes on His servants' lives. With Moses and Gideon, for example, in the Old Testament, or with Jesus calling His disciples, the pattern is that these men have a particular task. Moses is to lead the Israelites out of Egypt; Gideon to free them from the Midianites; and the disciples to become Jesus' apprentices (although at this early stage they can have little idea what that will entail).

Isaiah's experience is different. First comes a general call: "Whom shall I send?" Where? To do what? When? Isaiah knows no details whatever. This call doesn't come with a job description; there's no fine print for him to read before signing up. Yet here's the striking thing: he accepts the call anyway. He's like someone volunteering for the military, who undertakes to go on any mission, whatever the commanding officer decrees.

What brought Isaiah to the point where he could so unhesitatingly sign a contract whose details God will fill in later? One factor is the vision he has experienced of God's holiness. Read verses 1-4 in this chapter to get a sense of what he saw. The vision led him to realize his utter unworthiness to be in God's presence, let alone feel qualified to serve Him. God's holiness has shown up his sinfulness.

The second factor is the solution to that problem: "Then one of the seraphim flew to me with a live coal in his hand, which he had taken with tongs from the altar. With it he touched my mouth and said, 'See, this has touched your lips; your guilt is taken away and your sin atoned for.'" (Verses 6-7) Thus cleansed, Isaiah was now freed and equipped for kingly service, whatever the task.

Centuries later, John the Baptist "…saw Jesus coming toward him and said, 'Look, the Lamb of God, who takes away the sin of the world!'" (Jn. 1:29) Now, it is not only one man being cleansed and equipped for an as-yet unspecified life of service, it is *all* of us who see Jesus as our Lord. And like Isaiah, we too are now able to say, "Here am I. Send me."

6: Mary — The Lord's Servant

Read Luke 1:26-38

<u>Key Verse</u>: *"'I am the Lord's servant,' Mary answered. 'May your word to me be fulfilled.' Then the angel left her." (Verse 38)*

This may be a gross generalization, but Protestants tend to think Catholics go overboard in their adulation of Mary. Catholics, on the other hand, think Protestants don't give Mary nearly the respect and honor that she deserves. Wherever the truth lies, one thing is beyond dispute: Mary features in Scripture as a unique servant of the Lord because of her readiness to be Jesus' mother.

Women readers of this book, especially those who are mothers, can relate to Mary in a way that men cannot. Men have no idea what it must be like to know you have a person growing inside of you, slowly forcing changes in your body and culminating in a delivery typically accompanied by excruciating pain. Then, that pain is offset by the arrival of a wrinkled, crying, blood- and fluid-covered little person, the fruit of your body.

But even the mothers among us cannot grasp what Mary experienced when the angel Gabriel said, in those cryptic words: "The Holy Spirit will come on you, and the power of the Most High will overshadow you." (Lk. 1:35) How can she as a virgin conceive? However she understood Gabriel's words, Mary's unhesitating response is to tell the angel that she accepts this mysterious assignment. Unlike Zechariah, whose questions are rooted in skepticism, Mary's bewilderment isn't tainted with disbelief; hers is an honest question about how she would become pregnant.

Why does she accept this assignment? Because, as she says, "I am the Lord's servant." She is well aware of the implications for the social standing of being an unmarried mother in a conservative community, to say nothing of her relationship with Joseph. Being pregnant out of wedlock was both a moral and a legal offense. In other words, acquiescing to this unprecedented assignment came with considerable risk.

There will likewise be the gossip in the community for her to deal with. The stigma doesn't go away. When Jesus is a grown man and returns to Nazareth after being away preaching and teaching, Mark tells us how the townspeople responded. They asked scornfully, "Isn't this the carpenter? Isn't this Mary's son...?" (Mk. 6:3) Not *Joseph's* son, mind you. Typically, descent was described through the father's line. But not here, where instead the pointed reference to Mary is a reminder of that out-of-wedlock scandal from thirty years ago.

Aside from the social price she would pay on accepting this charge, Mary suffered the anguish of nurturing a son whose character and demeanor seemed mysteriously beyond her understanding. The gap between the two of them must have widened greatly once He began His preaching and teaching ministry. Then three years later came the horror of the crucifixion, with the agony that no mother should ever bear.

Yet God chose *her* to be His servant. Why, of all people? Because, as Gabriel says, she has found favor with God. It is clear from her response and her subsequent prayer, which we know as the Magnificat or Mary's song (Lk. 1:46-55), that despite her youth she was spiritually ready for this life-changing — and in fact *history*-changing — event. Her song, according to the *New Bible Commentary*, "... express[es] the state of her soul and reveals the high spiritual plane on which she had been living."[20]

For us today, perhaps the two most important lessons to be learned from Mary's servant heart are the need for spiritual preparedness and unhesitating obedience to God's call, however it might come. Mary had no doubt whatever that Gabriel's presence and message were real. Confirming his message was the miraculous pregnancy of her cousin Elizabeth, who had been barren. A state of spiritual preparedness isn't a precondition for hearing God's call; think of Saul on the road to Damascus, for example. He was openly resistant and hostile to the gospel message. But God spoke to him despite that. Mostly, though, we need to be as spiritually ready as we can for whatever message or assignment God might have for us.

Then, as we see with numerous other servants we'll meet in this book, an unquestioning obedience to that call is in order. We could call it a "faithful alacrity," with alacrity meaning an eager or enthusiastic promptness in our response.

The New Jerome Commentary says, "Mary of Nazareth is the model believer and slave who responds wholeheartedly to God's plan and is the forerunner of Luke's rogues' gallery, i.e. women, sinners, 'little people' whom no one would expect to respond favorably to God's revelation."[21]

Mary takes God at His word, like Abraham not understanding why God wanted him to sacrifice Isaac, or Noah going ahead with his ark construction when there wasn't a cloud in sight. "I am the Lord's servant," she says, adding the "yes" that leads to our Savior's conception.

What greater act of servanthood could there be?

---

[20] *New Bible Commentary*, 843.
[21] *The New Jerome Commentary*, 681.

7: Moses — The Chosen Servant

Read Exodus 14

Key Verse: *"And when the Israelites saw the mighty hand of the LORD displayed against the Egyptians, the people feared the LORD and put their trust in him and in Moses his servant." (Verse 31)*

Someone said of Moses that he spent forty years thinking he was somebody, forty years thinking he was a nobody, and forty years learning what God could do with a nobody.

And what a wonder-work God did with Moses, making this initially reluctant servant into a man who became the towering spiritual and political leader of the children of Israel, securing their release from slavery and getting them to the border of the Promised Land.

Of all the perils and triumphs of that journey, the undoubted pinnacle was the crossing of the Red Sea, the most vivid act of rescue by which God saved His people at the beginning of their flight from Egypt. Other acts of rescue followed during their four decades in the wilderness, such as water when they needed it, along with manna and quail. But the parting of the Red Sea was seared into the consciousness of the children of Israel and was central to their collective identity as God's chosen people.

Then there was Moses: the man saved as an infant from the river Nile, educated in the Egyptian court, guilty of impulsively murdering an Egyptian slave driver, driven to exile, and then called by God, via a burning bush that mysteriously wouldn't stop burning, to go and demand of Pharaoh the release of his work force.

Moses is hardly an eager volunteer for the task, as we know from his exchanges with God at the burning bush, with him offering one excuse after another. Moses' objections culminate in what sounds like a line from a TV comedy sketch, when he pitifully acknowledges he's run out of excuses and says, "Pardon your servant, Lord. Please send someone else." (Ex. 4:13) He's saying both that he's God's servant but that he won't serve. No enthusiastic "I'll-be-your-server-tonight" thinking from the man who becomes the greatest of leaders — or, more accurately, the greatest of servant leaders.

As we look back on his life, what qualities did God see in this hesitant man that made him a superb choice for rescuing His people from slavery? We can identify at least five qualities that made him a leader — but also a servant — par excellence.

His Openness to Learning: We've already noted his hesitancy when God first calls him via the burning bush. But to his great credit, he doesn't stay a reluctant leader. Even though it may be grudging at first, he finally succumbs to God's summons to leadership and a unique servant role. As we see in the rest of Exodus, he grows into the role, accepting his duties with increasing confidence.

He is no dictator but is humble enough to learn from others. Take for example the episode involving Jethro, his father-in-law. (Ex. 18:13-27) When Jethro enters the picture and notices how overwhelmed Moses is in settling disputes among the Israelites, he offers concrete suggestions regarding the art of delegation. Moses follows his advice and gives a group of God-fearing, capable, and honest men the training they need to take over the bulk of the disputes. They are to bring only the most difficult cases to Moses. He realizes that he can better serve God under this new arrangement.

His Boldness: For a man who committed murder decades before, it takes considerable courage to show up in the Egyptian court and demand an audience with Pharaoh. The cheek of it: Here's this refugee from the Egyptian court, who impetuously murdered an Egyptian overseer and then went on to become a shepherd, and now has the gall to enter the presence of the most powerful man in the country and tell him what to do.

The Egyptian leader could have him arrested and jailed. Instead, he listens to the Moses and Aaron duo. He initially refuses their request but then agrees to let the people go, before changing his mind. Pharaoh's anger and frustration increase as one plague after another afflicts him and his people, and he begins to grasp the power of the God whom Moses and Aaron represent. Moses is empowered by God's promises and presence as he returns to Pharaoh's court time after time, demanding the release of the Israelites.

Moses' boldness is seen too in the way he persists in calling on Pharaoh, even when the Israelites see their plight worsen when Pharaoh requires them to gather their own straw to make bricks. The people are furious with Moses, understandably so. He turns to God in frustration, but God again assures His servant that Pharaoh will free the Israelites. In brief, time and again, while still in Egypt and after their exodus, Moses comes to God and is emboldened and encouraged. He is learning what God can do with a nobody.

His Meekness: Our contemporary understanding of meekness has unfortunately been tainted and we think of it as sappiness and weakness. We miss the heart of what Jesus is getting at when in the beatitudes He says, "Blessed are the meek, for they shall inherit the earth." (Mt. 5:5) There's a Charles Wesley hymn that begins "Gentle Jesus, Meek and Mild." Or there's this assessment by Dorothy Sayers, who lamented the way the modern church portrays Jesus: "We have efficiently pared the claws of the Lion of Judah, certified him 'meek and mild' and recommended him as a fitting household pet for pale curates and pious old ladies."[22]

That was never the Jesus of the New Testament. Nor was it the Moses of the Old. E. M. Blaiklock says that Moses' chief characteristic was meekness, which he describes as follows:

> *Meekness is not insensibility or servility, and there was no call for him to demean himself before the crowd. Meekness does not cringe. It is benevolent, patient, forbearing, quiet. Like love, its basic element is that it "bears all things." Meekness has its active and passive elements. It leads to the subduing of wrath and resentment, and bearing the resentment of others.*[23]

Blaiklock adds that Moses falls short of this ideal when he loses his temper in yet another showdown with his people, as we'll see presently. For the most part, though, this man models the qualities that make up Blaiklock's description of meekness. Moses' servanthood is characterized in particular by his persistence, to which we now turn.

His Persistence: Leading the children of Israel must have been like herding cats, puppies, and a drove of stubborn donkeys all at once. Time and again, this group of former slaves whines and grumbles, sometimes for good reason. Yet the trust they display in following Moses out of Egypt, no longer slaves and laden with riches they took from their Egyptian oppressors, soon evaporates. When they see Pharaoh and his army approaching behind, with the Red Sea in front of them, "They said to Moses, 'Was it because there were no graves in Egypt that you brought us to the desert to die? What have you done to us by bringing us out of Egypt?'" (Ex. 14:11) Then follows the miracle of the Red Sea parting before them.

Having escaped across the Red Sea, they rebel when water and food become scarce. Worst of all is their decision to make a golden calf as a god competing with Yahweh. Yet Moses sticks with these recalcitrant people, at times pleading on their behalf in his role as a mediator between them and a God whose patience they sorely try. For example, following the golden calf episode, God says, "Now leave me alone so that my anger may burn against them and that I may destroy them. Then I will make you into a great nation." (Ex. 32:10)

It's a tempting moment; as the *New International Version* study Bible notes, God is offering to end the legacy of Abraham and start a new people—"a great nation"—under Moses.

Yet Moses pleads for God to change His mind and spare the unruly, faithless mob, with the result that "the Lord relented and did not bring on his people the disaster he had threatened." (Ex. 32:14) Moses sticks with his people through it all, confirming Blaiklock's assessment that Moses'

---

[22] Quoted in Gordon S. Jackson: *Quotes for the Journey, Wisdom for the Way*, 99.
[23] E. M. Blaiklock: *Handbook of Bible People*, 96.

defining quality of meekness includes his being "benevolent, patient and forbearing."

His Unparalleled Faith in Yahweh: Moses has a profound relationship with God, more than anyone else in Scripture except perhaps Adam and Eve before the fall.[24] For here is a man with whom God speaks "face to face." This description comes after Aaron and the elders of Israel accompany Moses to the foot of the mountain, which he and Joshua ascend. Moses goes on to be alone with God for forty days. The account also tells us something quite extraordinary, that this group got to see the God of Israel: "Moses and Aaron, Nadab and Abihu [Aaron's sons], and the seventy elders of Israel went up and saw the God of Israel." (Ex. 24:9-10)

Commentators note that this must have been a partial vision or insight into God's glory, because elsewhere we're told that seeing God face to face would mean death. As God says a few chapters later, "You cannot see my face, for no one may see me and live." (Ex. 33:20) In verse 11 of this chapter we read that "The Lord would speak to Moses face to face, as one speaks to a friend." While this description testifies to the unique intimate relationship Moses had with God, even he could not have experienced the full glory of God's presence.

Following forty days on the mountain, Moses descends with the second set of the Ten Commandments, having broken the first in his anger over the golden calf worship that Aaron condoned. Following his second go at receiving the commandments, we read: "When Moses came down from Mount Sinai with the two tablets of the covenant law in his hands, he was not aware that his face was radiant because he had spoken with the LORD." (Ex. 34:29)

~~~~~

Clearly, an integral part of Moses' leadership and servanthood is his extraordinary relationship with Yahweh, as he faithfully carries out his role as God's servant. Always obedient to God's commands, he nevertheless still has traces of the temper that led him to murder the Egyptian in his distant past. His anger ultimately prevents him from entering the Promised Land.

The account in Numbers 20 of yet another rebellion by the Israelites leads Moses to inquire of God how to provide desperately needed water for the angry people. God tells him to speak to a rock. Instead, Moses loses his temper and strikes the rock with his staff, not just once but twice. Yes, water flows out and meets the people's needs. But Moses has through his rash act forfeited his right to complete this arduous journey with his people. Commentators suspect there's more going on regarding Moses' sin and the ensuing punishment, which seems extremely harsh to us. The writer has left us with no more information, however.

So we come to the end of his journey, with a sad story of a servant who

---

[24] And Jesus, of course.

has stumbled and incurred God's displeasure. We can only speculate on the reason underlying God's anger. Was it Moses' disobedience that led to this punishment? Or was it his lack of trust, as if he thought striking the rock was needed, not merely talking to it? Or was it somehow an insult to God, as the Lord says later, that he and Aaron "disobeyed my command to honor me as holy before their eyes." (Num. 27:14) The account of the original episode isn't clear how God's holiness was disrespected. We don't know precisely.

But we can learn two things from Moses' punishment. One is that even the most exemplary servants of God can stumble at times, sometimes disrupting their relationship with Him. The other is reassuring. It concerns Moses' subsequent appearance at Jesus' transfiguration, along with Elijah. In a way beyond our understanding, the three disciples witnessing the transfiguration saw these two heroes of the Old Testament continuing to serve and support the Lord even hundreds of years after their deaths.

When a Polish Jew, Rabbi Zusya, was facing death, he reportedly said: "In the coming world, they will not ask me, 'Why were you not Moses?' They will ask me, 'Why were you not Zusya?'"[25] None of us can be a Moses. Nor should we try. But Rabbi Zusya's challenge to each of us is to rise to whatever service God may present us, with the courage, persistence and faithfulness Moses modeled for all of us.

---

[25] https://www.goodreads.com/quotes/61799-before-his-death-rabbi-zusya-said-in-the-coming-world. Accessed Sept. 5, 2023.

8: Paul — The Battle-Scarred Servant

Read 2 Corinthians 11:23-28

Key Verse: *"Are they servants of Christ? ... I am more." (Verse 23)*

It is quite the list: repeated imprisonments, flogging, stoning, shipwreck, and more — all in the cause of Christ. At a time hardly known for its sensitivity to human rights or respectful treatment of one's opponents, Paul's often controversial message led to one violent attack after another.[26]

Suffering, then, is repeatedly associated with Paul, not only for himself but potentially for all Christians. Roger Mohrlang writes, "The theme of suffering runs through several of his letters (especially 2 Corinthians, Philippians, and 2 Timothy). He makes it clear to his converts that suffering is part of their calling as Christians."

Paul's courage in facing hostile crowds was astonishing. In Lystra, for example, he healed a lame man, a miracle that led the crowd to see him and Barnabus as gods. While trying to persuade the locals they were mere mortals, some Jews from Antioch and Iconium arrived and turned the crowd against Paul. They then stoned him and dragged him unconscious outside the city, leaving him for dead. But he regained consciousness and dared to return to the city, where he stayed the night with some disciples. The next day he and Barnabus left for Derbe. (Acts 14:8-20)

Without being reckless, Paul repeatedly faced death for the sake of the gospel. As he said in 2 Corinthians, he had been exposed to death again and again. (2 Cor. 11:23) Suffering bodily harm was inherent in Paul's ministry. As Mohrlang says, "The message Paul preaches is embodied in his own suffering."

There is another category of suffering that Paul endured, the well-known but vaguely described "thorn in the flesh." (2 Cor. 12:7-8) Some commentators think this may have been a chronic vision problem, resulting from his being blinded on the road to Damascus. Others suggest it may have been symbolic of a spiritual problem that he could not overcome. Regardless of the truth, it was significant enough for him (1) to mention it at all, and (2) to say its severity helped to keep him humble. Presumably it was debilitating and prevented him from engaging in his ministry as fully as he would have liked.

Paul saw himself as an apostle, called by Jesus Himself to preach the

---

[26] Parts of this Profile are based on Roger Mohrlang's study, *Paul and his Life-Transforming Theology* (Eugene, Oregon: 2013).

gospel. In his preaching, he was not only courageous. He was faithful, passionate and articulate in taking the good news to the Gentile world. A brilliant theologian, he was flexible but not wishy-washy in how he presented the gospel to different audiences. As he told the Corinthians:

> *To the Jews I became like a Jew, to win the Jews. To those under the law*
> *I became like one under the law (though I myself am not under the law),*
> *so as to win those under the law. To those not having the law I became*
> *like one not having the law (though I am not free from God's law but am*
> *under Christ's law), so as to win those not having the law. To the weak*
> *I became weak, to win the weak. I have become all things to all people so*
> *that by all possible means I might save some. (1 Cor. 9:20-22)*

But Paul also saw himself as a servant. Toward the end of his ministry, while in prison in Caesarea, he was granted an audience with King Agrippa, who was keen to hear Paul's story first-hand. So he recounted his dramatic conversion story to a new audience, saying what Jesus told him in that cataclysmic moment en route to Damascus: "I have appeared to you to appoint you as a servant and as a witness of what you have seen and will see of me." (Acts 26:16)

What a servant he became. Mohrlang says, "Among the early Christians, Paul was truly remarkable. His contribution to the Christian faith, both as a missionary-evangelist and as a letter writer, was monumental." Just as he spoke to the Jews as a Jew, or to those under the law as one under the law, so too his legacy as one of God's premier servants speaks to us today.

9: Samuel — The Listening Servant

Read 1 Samuel 3

<u>Key Verse</u>: *"The LORD came and stood there, calling as at the other times, 'Samuel! Samuel!' Then Samuel said, 'Speak, for your servant is listening.'" (Verse 10)*

This chapter describing a confused young boy, an old has-been priest, and a persistent God is packed with meaning. It is the calling of a child whose previously barren mother miraculously conceived and dedicated him to the Lord's service. He is mentored by an aging priest, Eli, who increasingly realizes the time is coming for a changing of the guard, and that he will forfeit his role as God's representative to his protégé.

What concerns us in this Profile are not the ramifications of Samuel's ascent to becoming one of Israel's most formidable and influential figures and one of God's preeminent servants. Rather, we will look at the specifics surrounding the call of this young boy.

Three times in Chapter 3 the boy hears a voice calling his name. It is nighttime and he understandably assumes the aging Eli is seeking help. Yet each time he hears the voice of the Lord, which Eli finally realizes, and tells the boy, "Go and lie down, and if he calls you, say, 'Speak, LORD, for your servant is listening.'" Then the voice comes a fourth time, and Samuel responds, "Speak, for your servant is listening."

Let us comment briefly on the curious anomaly between Eli's instruction to Samuel — "Say 'Speak, LORD, for your servant is listening'" — and Samuel's actual response. Why does Samuel not address the LORD? One possible explanation is his uncertainty if this was in fact Yahweh speaking to him. After all, we learned in verse 7 that Samuel does not yet know the Lord. He has not previously heard His voice. Another is that he *does* realize this voice is Yahweh's and is thoroughly intimidated. Or he refrains from saying LORD, or "Yahweh," out of reverence. In verse 10 we read the strange statement that the Lord came and stood there, possibly as an apparition that might have terrified the boy. Or perhaps there's yet another explanation. The main point of the exchange, however, is that Samuel affirms two things: that he is "Your servant" and that he is listening.

What are we to learn from this series of encounters that introduce us to God's listening servant? First, Samuel is in a good place to hear God's call. He is in the Lord's house, by the Ark of the Covenant. He is in a holy place, close to holy things. Certainly, God can speak to us no matter where we are. As Matthew Henry says, "No place excludes divine visits."[27] But we are more likely to be receptive to His word in a cathedral than a nightclub. Samuel, already in the service of the Lord, is thus predisposed to this divine encounter.

A second lesson may seem obvious, but it is nevertheless crucial: God's call requires a response. So, even though Samuel gets it wrong three times, thinking it is Eli who's calling him, he is on the right track. We too may mistake signals in our lives that are in fact God prodding us into some course of action. Or even worse, we may ignore the signals completely. As we ought always to be listening for the prompting of the Holy Spirit in our lives, we should be careful not to preclude the ways in which God might be talking to us.

Third, sometimes we need to hear God's message several times before it gets through to us. Be alert, therefore, to what may look like coincidences that keep cropping up, which seem to suggest we should be doing something, like considering a career change, for example.

Fourth, it may be that we think we're hearing God's call, perhaps regarding that possible career change. But things seem unclear and murky. Maybe the intervention of our own Eli is needed, someone who can help interpret what we're hearing. An objective outsider whose spiritual wisdom you trust may be able to help you distinguish between what could be the Holy Spirit's prompting, or a bad case of indigestion.

Finally, listening well to God is good; what you hear, though, might not be. Poor Samuel now becomes the conveyor of harsh and grim news to his mentor. He is the messenger who brings bad tidings, delivering a slap in the face to Eli—to whom God has something to say. God doesn't speak to Eli directly; He uses a young boy who until the previous night had never even heard God's voice. But now he is a servant who has undergone his first lesson in listening to the Almighty.

---

[27] Matthew Henry: *One-Volume Commentary on the Bible*, 48.

PART 3: THE SERVANTS WE MAY RECOGNIZE

10: Bilhah and Zilpah — The Surrogate Servants

Read Genesis 30:1-3

Key Verse: *"Then she said, 'Here is Bilhah, my servant. Sleep with her so that she can bear children for me and I too can build a family through her.'" (Verse 3)*

By the end of Genesis Chapter 30, Jacob must have been exhausted. Here he was, begetting (to use King James English) sons one after another, with his two wives and their surrogates. We'll concentrate here on Bilhah, Rachel's maid, whom we first meet in the previous chapter. Bilhah is a servant of Rachel's father, Laban. He gives her to Rachel as her attendant when Rachel marries Jacob. Having previously been tricked into marrying Rachel's sister Leah, Jacob commits to serving Laban for another seven years to win Rachel as his bride.

While Rachel and Leah, and Laban and Jacob, are the central figures in the story, Bilhah's role as a surrogate mom is important too. We most likely find the idea of this kind of surrogacy uncomfortable or downright troubling. Women generally were regarded in this culture as chattel, little more than breeding machines. The status of a maid like Bilhah is even lower; she is in a slave-like role, subject even to having to sleep with her mistress' husband. Any children she might have are "attributed" to her mistress. This practice was not without precedent in the Genesis account; Sarah, desperate for children, gave her maid, Hagar, to Abraham to conceive on her behalf.

The *King James Version* has an odd expression in verse 1: offering her maid to Jacob, Rachel says, "go in unto her; and she shall bear upon my knees, that I may also have children by her." What's with the knees? The *Catholic Bible's* study note explains: "In the ancient Near East, a father would take a newborn child in his lap to signify that he acknowledged it as his own. Rachel uses this ceremony in order to adopt the child and establish her legal rights to it."[28] Bilhah, then, forsakes all rights to a child she has carried for nine months. It is difficult to imagine a more demanding role of a servant than this: bear a child on someone else's behalf, a child to whom you will have no rights.

Bilhah's contribution, however, is indispensable in addressing Rachel's barrenness, which was a cause of intense anguish in a culture

---

[28] *The Catholic Bible*, 36.

where, as we have seen, women's role was preeminently that of child bearers. In verse 1, she cries to her husband to give her children or she "will die." Aggravating the situation is that her sister, Leah, is bearing children. The longstanding hostility between the two sisters spills over to their respective maids. Not only is Bilhah brought in to bear children on Rachel's behalf, Leah also turns to surrogacy when it seems she can no longer conceive. So Jacob gets to know Zilpah in a more personal way, and she too conceives. Later, we learn that the firstborn son, Reuben, ends up sleeping with Bilhah. We are given no more details beyond the fact of this shameful encounter. The writer makes no attempt to shield us from the tensions and dysfunctional relations in Jacob's household. Few episodes in Scripture have such a soap opera feel to them. As Matthew Henry notes, "There was much amiss in the contest and competition between these two sisters." Yet, he adds, "God brought good out of this evil."[29]

So too with us, when things aren't going well. It could be a sudden health crisis or a business deal gone badly wrong. Or maybe you're facing a serious legal issue or are the victim of a great wrong, a situation from which you see no escape. Whatever your circumstances, Matthew Henry's words offer great consolation. We are reminded that God always, *always*, has the power to bring "good out of this evil."

Which brings us back to Bilhah and Zilpah. Amidst the messiness of a Middle Eastern family about three millennia ago, two otherwise obscure women each gave birth to two of Jacob's sons, thus providing the lineage of a quarter of the tribes of Israel. No insignificant contribution, that.

---

[29] Matthew Henry: *One-Volume Commentary on the Bible*, 50.

11: Caleb and Joshua — The Outvoted Servants

Read Numbers 13:30-31

<u>Key Verse</u>: *"Then Caleb silenced the people before Moses and said, 'We should go up and take possession of the land, for we can certainly do it.'" (Verse 30)*

It was all a matter of perspective. Caleb and Joshua, with ten others, had spied out the Promised Land over forty days. They had seen exactly the same things: the richness of the land, "flowing with milk and honey," and abundant fruit. Sent out to serve Moses as spies, to assess the viability of possessing the land, they brought back grapes, pomegranates, and figs as evidence.

But while Caleb and Joshua saw opportunity, the other ten spies were overwhelmed and intimidated by the inhabitants, beside whom they felt "like grasshoppers." Based on identical experiences and the same evidence, how could Caleb and Joshua have differed so markedly from the others? F. B. Meyer says, "They saw the same spectacles in their survey of the land; but the result in the one case was *panic*, in the other *confidence and peace*. What made the difference? It lay in this, that the ten spies compared themselves with the giants, whilst the two compared the giants with God."[30]

This was an early version of seeing the glass as either half full or half empty. Looking at the situation with a faith-filled perspective, Caleb and Joshua gave a positive report. They were overridden, however, by the ten. This lost opportunity for entering the Promised Land imposed on the Israelites another forty years of wandering the desert. As Numbers 15:37 indicates each of the ten spies died in a plague. As a result, only Caleb and Joshua made it into the Promised Land, thanks to the votes they cast that fateful day — votes of confidence in God's plans for the children of Israel.

In the long run (that is, a forty-year run) their votes were honored, as was the undercover mission they conducted. Their service as spies on Moses' behalf was finally recognized and they alone of the original group made it across the Jordan.

Sometimes Christians have a tough time with God's timetable and wish He would hurry things along. When we read in Revelation that He promises to "make all things new," (Rev. 21:5, *King James Version*) we often find ourselves saying, "But *when*?"

---

[30] Quoted in <u>https://enduringword.com/bible-commentary/numbers-13/</u>. Accessed Sept. 5, 2023.

Time to heed the advice of Stephen Merritt, who warned: "Cease meddling with God's plans and will... You may move the hands of a clock, but you do not change the time; so you may hurry the unfolding of God's will, but you harm and may not help the work."[31]

The apostle Peter points to the gap between our handle on time and that of the One who transcends time as we know it: "With the Lord a day is like a thousand years and a thousand years are like a day." (2 Pet. 3:8) In ways we cannot conceive, He is able, and willing, to endure an unimaginably long labor to bring to birth these "new things," to match His perfect timing. And while He does so, He expects us to continue serving Him to the utmost.

Just like Caleb and Joshua.

[31] https://www.dailychristianquote.com/stephen-merritt/. Accessed Sept. 5, 2023.

12: Cornelius' Servants — The Gentile Servants

Read Acts 10

<u>Key Verses</u>: *"When the angel who spoke to him had gone, Cornelius called two of his servants and a devout soldier who was one of his attendants. He told them everything that had happened and sent them to Joppa." (Verses 7-8)*

Cornelius' two servants and devout soldier play a far greater part in the history of the still-fledgling Christian church than they could possibly have imagined. Their role is central to the "story about the first time a Gentile was publicly and officially welcomed into the Christian fellowship without conforming to the requirements of the Jewish law," says *The Interpreter's Bible*. "It marks the point at which Christianity dramatically and decisively asserted its independence of Judaism."[32]

Cornelius' vision is so compelling that he cannot dismiss it and does what he's told. In keeping with the angel's instructions, he sends this delegation to Joppa to find this fellow named Simon, also called Peter. Why the soldier? Several possible reasons come to mind. One is to provide security for the servants. Another is to lend authority to the unusual request they will make of Peter. Neither Cornelius nor his delegation knows anything about Peter, or his possible receptivity to Cornelius' request. But the fact that a Roman soldier shows up would make anyone take seriously the message they bring. A third, but probably less likely, explanation is that the soldier would compel Peter to come with them — maybe not in as many words but with an unmistakable hint. ("Now you wouldn't want to deny my friends' request that you come with us, would you? We soldiers don't like being defied, know what I mean?") No, almost certainly not — because of the character of this particular soldier, one who we are told is "devout." Cornelius doesn't choose this man by chance. The fact that he is a soldier *and* devout is a significant combination.

But God first needs to destroy Peter's assumption about the Gentiles, as we see in one of the most ironic passages in Scripture. In verse 14, when God tells Peter to eat the unclean foods he sees in his vision, he responds: "Surely not, Lord!" He contradicts God and calls Him "Lord" in the same breath. The vision has a profound impact on him; twice we are told that he ponders its meaning. He is still doing so when the Holy Spirit tells him that three men are looking for him and that he should go with them.

---

[32] *The Interpreter's Bible*, vol. 9, 133.

That's an important aspect of the messengers' role that is worth noting: The Holy Spirit has gone ahead of them, facilitating their mission. As Eugene Peterson says, reflecting on his duties as a pastor: "We are always coming in on something that is already going on... Always we are dealing with what the risen Christ has already set in motion."[33]

If the Spirit had wanted, He could merely have told Peter to go to Cornelius, without the need for these messengers and thus sparing them the thirty-four-mile journey from Caesarea to Joppa. Because the three men have no idea how the Spirit has been preparing Peter for their arrival, they may be surprised when he readily accepts their invitation to return with them to their master. He invites them to stay the night, violating the taboo that Jews should keep their distance from Gentiles. This offer of hospitality is the first tangible step demonstrating Peter's radical new openness to Gentiles, those whom he formerly saw as "unclean."

There's much more to be said about the vital importance of this development in the life of the church. But our interest here is with the three messengers and it is to them we must return. The next day they return to Caesarea, together with the apostle and some believers from Joppa whom Peter has recruited. Cornelius' messengers succeed in their mission to return with Peter, the one person whose credibility and standing in the church is essential in persuading the young church that the gospel is intended for the Gentiles as well as the Jews.

We are told nothing else about Cornelius' three emissaries. But we can deduce from Acts Chapter 9 that these men were dependable and trustworthy. It is hard to imagine how powerful Cornelius' vision must have been, and he needed men to follow the Spirit's instructions and do exactly what he told them. We can further assume that they were in good enough shape physically to undertake this journey. Certainly, the soldier would have been, but Cornelius would have chosen only servants who were up to an arduous journey, presumably on horseback. In addition, he would have ensured they were suitably equipped. The soldier would have had his weapons; between them they would have had food and probably some money to pay for lodging if they needed that.

We can be confident that the three messengers were among the large gathering to whom Peter spoke on his arrival at Cornelius' house. It is inconceivable that after taking part in this unusual mission, marked by miraculous visions that both their master and this Jewish man had experienced, they would miss the opportunity to hear what Peter had to say. So we can assume that they were among those who were converted that day, receiving the Holy Spirit and subsequently baptism.

We too may serve as messengers in God's service, quite unaware of the stakes involved in our task. But as with Cornelius' messengers, we can be

---

[33] Eugene Peterson, *Living The Message*, Sept. 18.

assured that we will be suitably equipped for whatever assignments we undertake on God's behalf. We'll also be given whatever information or guidance we need to fulfill our mission. We can be sure too of an outcome no less in keeping with God's plans than what these three men experienced.

13: The Cupbearer and Joseph — The Symbiotic Servants

Read Genesis 40

Key Verse: *"The chief cupbearer, however, did not remember Joseph; he forgot him." (Verse 23)*

We could easily have a stand-alone Profile on Joseph, sold into slavery in an act of unspeakable cruelty by his brothers. He becomes an involuntary servant in the house of Potiphar, a wealthy Egyptian. Joseph's natural talents and integrity soon propel him to a leading servant role in the household. But after Potiphar's wife falsely accuses him of trying to rape her, he ends up in prison. Once again his abilities and character are recognized and in that setting too he rises to a trusted servant position.

The qualities Joseph displays in these situations reveal an astonishing resistance to the despair many of us would have embraced, in response to repeated injustices. Somehow, he transcends those wrongs, without turning his back on Yahweh. Indeed, his commitment not to wrong Potiphar or dishonor God finds an echo in prison, where he attributes his ability to interpret dreams to God.

It is in that prison setting where his path overlaps with the Pharaoh's butler, or cupbearer or chief steward. The cupbearer in ancient Middle East society was a senior official who had the ear of his master. His service typically included tasting the wine to ensure it wasn't poisoned, before presenting it to the ruler.

If anyone in Scripture can be seen as a pawn in God's hand, it would be the cupbearer. He has no idea how instrumental he will be in freeing Joseph from prison and, subsequently, empowering him to be the second-in-command of the entire country.

This senior Egyptian official is an integral player in the Joseph story, with his contribution to the unfolding of events summarized as follows:

- For reasons not mentioned in Scripture he angers Pharaoh, to the extent that he and the chief baker are thrown in jail.
- Then there's his odd dream, which Joseph — using his God-given gift of interpretation — explains, as he does for the hapless baker as well.
- As Joseph predicts, the cupbearer is restored to his position but he then conveniently forgets Joseph's plea to "mention me to Pharaoh and get me out of this prison."
- Two years later, when Pharaoh has his inexplicable and troubling

dreams, only then does the cupbearer remember the young Hebrew prisoner. The rest, as the cliché has it, is history.

~~~~~

Now, some details. Joseph befriends both the cupbearer and the baker, attending to them and noticing when they were troubled by their respective dreams. In keeping with his character, he has empathy for these men and on hearing what is upsetting them, uses the gift God had given him to interpret their dreams. One might hope that the official who gets out of jail alive would honor the request of this remarkable young man and tell Pharaoh of his wrongful imprisonment.

So much for gratitude. No, Joseph isn't responsible for freeing the cupbearer. But he does assuage his troubled soul by correctly interpreting his dream. This is an extraordinary accomplishment, all the more important in a culture that believed dreams foretold the future. Yet the powerful impression Joseph makes on him is soon forgotten.

The cupbearer continues in royal service, having for whatever reason put young Joseph out of his mind. While the cupbearer enjoys the luxury and power and perks that come with being a servant in Pharaoh's court, Joseph languishes in a dungeon. The days turn into months and the months into years. However, God has neither forgotten nor forsaken him.

As the cupbearer's apparent forgetfulness about Joseph is an important element in our story, we need to ask what lay behind it. Maybe it wasn't so much innocent forgetfulness as it was sheer indifference. Now that he is back in Pharaoh's good books, restored to favor, he no longer needs this young Hebrew and his uncanny gift for interpreting dreams. Nor does he care about the God to Whom Joseph gives credit for this gift, as we saw in verse 8.

What lessons can we learn from this self-serving servant of Pharaoh? What does Joseph's experience teach us? Let's begin with the cupbearer role. He is well trusted, at least until he incurs Pharaoh's displeasure. Again, for reasons we don't know, because of the ruler's birthday feast Pharaoh decides to restore the cupbearer to his former role. So he is on hand to mention Joseph and his gift of interpretation when all Pharaoh's other acolytes can't interpret his repeated dream.

As noted, it takes another two years before Joseph can taste the freedom he deserves, when the cupbearer finally remembers to mention Joseph's plight to Pharaoh — a step that would certainly help to increase his standing with this perplexed monarch. While he provides the solution to Pharaoh's needs, it certainly helps cement his previously shaky reputation in court.

Perhaps a more charitable assessment of the cupbearer's forgetfulness is in order. Maybe he did his best to erase his memory of the unhappy episode when he was in prison, especially given that his fellow prisoner was executed; that could easily have been him. The prison experience isn't something he wants on his resume.

Yet another charitable explanation may be that upon restoration to his position, the cupbearer is so caught up in his duties that the right moment for him to approach Pharaoh never arises. After all, one doesn't lightly approach as august a figure as the Pharaoh with what seems like a personal favor.

Whatever this man's motives or reasoning, Joseph's request lies dormant—until the time is ripe. God acts by jogging this royal servant's memory (or reawakening a sense of gratitude, perhaps), and he unwittingly triggers the chain of events that God had been planning all along. This is the same God of Whom the cupbearer had learned in a prison cell, and Whom he apparently promptly forgets as he turns his full attention to serving another master.

Let us end with Joseph's situation. If the cupbearer had brought Joseph's plight to Pharaoh immediately after regaining his freedom, and Joseph had been released, then what? What would he have been freed to? Surely he couldn't return to Potiphar's household. Would his slave status have consigned him to some other servant role in Egyptian society? Or perhaps the most optimistic scenario would be a get-out-of-jail free card, and a ticket back to his family in Canaan. If so, the crucial task God had lined up for him would go unfulfilled; Jacob and his eleven sons and their families may well have died in the upcoming famine, and the history we now have in the Old Testament would be unimaginably rewritten.

No, those extra two years were an essential aspect of God's overriding purposes. Paradoxically, the cupbearer who forgot or chose to suppress his prison experience or got too busy serving in the palace proved to be a far better servant in executing God's plan than he could possibly have known.

14: Doeg — The Massacring Servant

Read 1 Samuel 21-22

Key Verse: *"The king then ordered Doeg, 'You turn and strike down the priests.' So Doeg the Edomite turned and struck them down. That day he killed eighty-five men who wore the linen ephod." (Verse 22:18)*

If you'd prefer to skip today's reading of the two chapters in 1 Samuel, the three verses below will give you the *Reader's Digest* version of the events concerning Doeg. They give you the essence of this notorious servant of Saul, a man who betrayed David and then butchered eighty-five priests at Saul's command.

- *"Now one of Saul's servants was there that day, detained before the LORD; he was Doeg the Edomite, Saul's chief shepherd." (1 Sam. 21:7)*
- *"But Doeg the Edomite, who was standing with Saul's officials, said, "I saw the son of Jesse come to Ahimelek son of Ahitub at Nob." (1 Sam. 22:9)*
- *"The king then ordered Doeg, "You turn and strike down the priests." So Doeg the Edomite turned and struck them down. That day he killed eighty-five men who wore the linen ephod." (1 Sam. 22:18)*

The fuller version is that Doeg sees the refugee David fleeing from Saul and getting food from Ahimelek the priest. Interestingly, David lies to the priest about being on a special mission for Saul. Doeg witnesses Ahimelek's help to David and his men, and later tells Saul what he saw. Because Saul thinks Ahimelek has sided with David, he orders his guards to kill the priest. When they refuse, he turns to Doeg, who kills Ahimelek and eighty-five of his fellow priests.

By today's standards, both Saul and Doeg would be guilty of war crimes. To be fair, David too could be regarded in the same light. 1 Samuel 27:9, referring to the raids David conducted in Philistine territory while under the protection of the Philistine king, Achish, notes that, "Whenever David attacked an area, he did not leave a man or woman alive, but took sheep and cattle, donkeys and camels, and clothes."

But back to Doeg. Any argument that he was only following a superior's orders wouldn't wash at today's equivalent of a Nuremberg trial. His readiness to please his master by butchering the priests is compounded by his attack on their village. "He also put to the sword Nob, the town of the priests, with its men and women, its children and infants, and its cattle, donkeys and sheep." (1 Sam. 22:19)

Leon Uris (1923-2004) was an American writer best known for his novels. In one of them, *Armageddon: A Novel of Berlin* (1963), he describes one aspect of how Nazi SS officers were trained. They were each given a puppy to raise, supposedly to help the recruits learn discipline. Then, after several months, each recruit was abruptly ordered to kill his puppy. If they showed any hesitation, they were ousted from the program.

Doeg would have done well as an SS officer recruit. In his commentary, David Payne writes of Doeg's conduct that he is:

> ... *a man without pity or compunction. Where Saul's other courtiers were understandably very unwilling to attack Ahimelek and the other priests, Doeg showed no hesitation. His single-minded devotion was not to duty nor to Saul, but to himself and his own interests. We do not hear more of him, but no doubt he was duly rewarded by Saul for all he had done.*[34]

Servants, then, are not always good people. In the service of an evil person, duty becomes shameful, not honorable. For Christians, Doeg provides the prototypical example of misguided, malevolent service. We have much to learn from his perverse example.

---

[34] David Payne: *1 & 2 Samuel*, 118.

15: Eliezer — The Exemplary Servant

Read Genesis 24

Key Verse: *"Then he prayed, 'LORD, God of my master Abraham, make me successful today, and show kindness to my master Abraham.'" (Verse 12)*

We begin with an assumption: That the unidentified servant in Genesis 24 is in fact named Eliezer. In Genesis 15:2 Abram (who is not yet renamed as Abraham) tells Yahweh of his lack of an heir, despite God's promise to him. As things stand, Abram says, his senior servant will inherit everything on Abram's death, not the son who had been promised but who still had not arrived on the scene. That senior servant is identified as Eliezer of Damascus. The prominent figure in Chapter 24 is highly likely to be this same individual. So that's how we will refer to him from here on.

If you haven't yet read Chapter 24, the short version is that Abraham sends Eliezer to find a wife for Isaac (who has most definitely arrived on the scene and is now a grown man, ready to marry). But Abraham doesn't want a daughter-in-law from the locals and sends Eliezer to his "own country," to seek a wife for Isaac from Abraham's kin. The servant is made to take a vow that he will undertake this solemn mission. Through a practical test, he identifies Rebekah as the answer to his earnest prayer, and after meeting with her family and persuading them that this is of God, he begins his return journey with a bride for his master's son.

The main point of this chapter is how God provides the heir Abraham needs if God's promise to make him a great nation is to be fulfilled. But our focus is instead on Eliezer, the exemplary servant. Why exemplary? We'll identify nine reasons, which taken together make him a model of servanthood. Each of these nine considerations applies directly to our role as Christians today.

1. His trustworthiness. Finding a bride for Isaac is crucial to Abraham's need for a grandson, to help fulfill the promise God has made. So he turns to Eliezer, his most senior servant, to help accomplish this task. Abraham indicates the seriousness of this assignment by requiring the servant to take a vow; this is no ordinary master-servant interaction.

Abraham commits the endeavor to God and assures Eliezer that an angel will go ahead of him to pave the way for his success. As Abraham's most senior and trusted servant, Eliezer can be confident that his godly master's assurance is not to be taken lightly. He accepts the commission with a confidence that corresponds to the trust that Abraham places in him.

God in turn entrusts to us His work; we are His hands and feet. The story is told that when Jesus returned to heaven after His ascension and the angels asked Him what His plans were now, Jesus replied, "I've entrusted My team of disciples to spread the gospel message throughout the world."

"But what if that doesn't work?" the angels asked. "What is Your Plan B?"

"I have no plan B," Jesus said.

Such is His trust in us to carry on His work that He stakes it all on us.

2. A Realistic Response. Eliezer's first response is reasonable enough: He asks, "What if she's unwilling? What is Plan B?" He doesn't quibble with the order itself. Nor does he ask for more direction on what, on the face of it, seems a pretty tall order: arrive as a complete stranger and say you've come to play matchmaker for someone they've never seen. But Abraham's restated concern is that Eliezer not take Isaac back to the land of Abraham's family. Isaac is to stay in the Promised Land, to which God has brought Abraham, if His promise is to be fulfilled and Abraham will father a great nation.

Like Moses, Eliezer raises concerns about the mission to which he has been called. Moses' questions, though, as we read in Profile 7, were all excuses that culminated in him telling God, with great irony: "Pardon Your servant, Lord. Please send someone else." What kind of servant calls his master "Lord" and adds, "I won't do it; send someone with more courage/with better skills/with the right major in college." We too are entitled to ask Eliezer- and Moses-like questions, so long as they are clarifications of God's directions, and not excuses that amount to "No, Lord."

3. Into Action. Having clarified his master's expectations Eliezer sets out. He takes "with him ten of his master's camels loaded with all kinds of good things from his master." He has the authority to put together quite an entourage, a set of supplies, and whatever gifts he thinks might be needed if his mission turns out well. If Abraham had a credit card, Eliezer would have taken that too, knowing he had full spending authority of his master's money. Eliezer knows Abraham well enough that he draws on his master's supplies without having to ask. Also, he is clearly optimistic that this mission will succeed, or at least optimistic enough to prepare for the outcome Abraham desires.

Likewise with us today. We can be sure that God will not send us on assignment unprepared or ill-equipped. As Matthew Henry wrote, "God knows what he designs us for, that we be furnished with grace sufficient. He that appoints what the voyage shall be, will victual [supply] the ship accordingly."[35]

4. The Destination. There's the old joke about the fellow who's dropped his keys but instead of looking for them where they fell, he looks

---

[35] Matthew Henry: *One-Volume Commentary on the Bible*, 391.

under the lamppost a hundred yards away because the light is better there. Eliezer, by contrast, blends faith with common sense, and heads to what logically seems like a good place to find the answer: Aram Naharaim, or Northwest Mesopotamia, and the town of Nahor. He uses his head to heighten the chances of finding a solution while relying on his heart to trust in God to find a wife for Isaac.

5. Power of Prayer. The story skips details of the journey. No doubt it included at least some armed security men to protect an obviously wealthy group that was vulnerable to attacks by bandits. Then, on arrival at his destination, he prays: "…give me success today, and show kindness to my master Abraham." Given the example of deep faith he had seen in his master, Eliezer presumably had prayed frequently since setting out on this mission. Now, he prays again for his success, but not his own sake; instead he seeks Yahweh's "kindness" to his master.

Our work and ministry as Christians ought similarly to be focused on advancing God's Kingdom and His purposes. Success in our endeavors is good and well, but apart from God's will it is meaningless. Joseph Bayly said, "I know that any success apart from Your Spirit is mere euphemism for failure."[36]

6. Getting Practical. Now Eliezer does something similar to Gideon's use of a fleece to determine God's will. He gets extremely practical in using the "water for the camels" test. Unlike Gideon, though, he is not acting out of fear or insecurity. Eliezer is instead trusting God to show him, one way or another, the next step in his quest. Normally, we can't expect such clarity in the way God guides. But Eliezer's prayer is blessed both with clarity and immediacy as he gets God's direction.

7. Acceptance and Confirmation. Off he and Rebekah go to Bethuel's house, where Laban and Bethuel also recognize this development as having God's fingerprints all over it. As they say, "This is from the Lord; we can say nothing to you one way or another." With this affirmation that Rebekah is to be Isaac's wife, Eliezer gratefully accepts God's answer to his earlier prayer for success.

8. Implementation. But Eliezer's work isn't done. Having gained the consent of Rebekah's family for her to leave her home and become the wife of a man she'd never met, Eliezer encounters the family's request to stay longer. But he doesn't pull back from implementing his new-found answer. Rather than delaying, he overrides the request for Rebekah to stay longer. His stated goal is "that I may go to my master." Again, his focus is on serving Abraham, and by extension Isaac as well.

For us today the lesson is plain: Once we know God's will for our lives, we risk all if we deviate from the plan — especially if circumstances have made clear this is God's will. We can't know what Laban's motive was in

---

[36] Joseph Bayly: *Psalms of My Life*, 28.

wanting Rebekah to stay. Perhaps he is having second thoughts about her departure. Perhaps he wants to have a few more days with her before a departure that was final; he is unlikely ever to see her again. Eliezer, though, insists on carrying out God's purposes, and returning home. Now.

9. Completion. As Eliezer and the entourage approach Abraham's homestead, we have the poignant description of Rebekah asking him, "Who is that man in the field coming to meet us?" It is Isaac, and the servant responds, "He is my master." He serves both Abraham and Isaac. Then, we learn, "the servant told Isaac all he had done."

~~~~~

So his duty was done. We know nothing more about how this godly, loyal and faithful servant continued to serve Abraham and Isaac. But this story alone provides us a marvelous example of biblical servanthood. Interestingly, as one scholar has pointed out, this is the longest single narrative in the patriarchal literature, one that offers us an extended insight into a remarkable servant.

Among the qualities we've identified above, here was a man who:

- Sought the clarification he needed, then
- Obeyed unhesitatingly;
- Prepared appropriately;
- Acted confidently;
- Prayed frequently (three times in this narrative); and
- Stayed focused on his assignment until its completion.

With hindsight, we can see that Eliezer played a crucial role in the unfolding of God's plan for the formation of the nation of Israel. Yet for whatever reason the writer purposefully doesn't identify Eliezer in this story. For despite his central role, he is not the point of the story. The glory must, as always, belong to the God who arranged the perfectly timed rendezvous between this savvy, unassuming servant and the beautiful bride-to-be and wife to Isaac, and prepared the hearts of her family to see God's hand at work.

Regardless of who this servant was, whether Eliezer or some other trusted and intensely loyal member of Abraham's household, E. M. Blaiklock says "He is a good man to know. With his act of efficient, sensitive and selfless service he disappears from history, but not from the approval of God."[37]

---

[37] E. M. Blaiklock: *Handbook of Bible People*, 34.

16: Elijah's Servant — The Weather Monitoring Servant

Read 1 Kings 18:1-46

<u>Key Verses</u>: *"'Go and look toward the sea,' he told his servant. And he went up and looked. 'There is nothing there,' he said. Seven times Elijah said, 'Go back.' The seventh time the servant reported, 'A cloud as small as a man's hand is rising from the sea.'" (Verses 43-44)*

The context for this servant's brief appearance in Scripture is Elijah's famous victory over the prophets of Baal on Mount Carmel. Elijah has thoroughly and spectacularly routed, and then slaughtered, these opponents of Yahweh. Now, he has one more miracle to introduce that will show the power of God: the arrival of rain that will break the drought and the ensuing famine referred to at the beginning of this chapter.

Elijah and this unidentified servant are on top of Mount Carmel. He tells the servant to go and look toward the sea. The servant reports that he can see nothing. Seven times Elijah orders him to do so. Finally, on that seventh foray he sees what verse 44 notes is "a cloud as small as a man's hand."

Such is the beginning of the end: the drought is broken and Yahweh's power is once again miraculously demonstrated in the land. Elijah's reputation as one of the greatest of Israel's prophets is reinforced.

But what of the servant, of whom we know nothing? Well, not quite nothing. We can identify at least four qualities of this individual, each of which should mark our discipleship today.

His courage: He is willing to associate with Elijah during the high-stakes showdown with the prophets of Baal. This is literally a life-and-death struggle between those prophets and Yahweh's representative. It doesn't end well for the Baal brigade. But Elijah's servant couldn't know that at the beginning of this encounter. He could easily have decided to cut and run but he sticks with Elijah.

His experience. After witnessing the miracles that Elijah performed in Yahweh's name, this servant is never the same. He has seen first-hand the power of Elijah's God. First, there's the altar soaked in water that gets struck by lightning. That's followed by the tiny cloud that grows into a downpour and breaks the prolonged drought, just as Elijah predicted. Quite possibly, he has seen other miracles that Elijah has performed. The Mount Carmel chapter, even by itself, provides a landmark on his faith journey, which he can always recall with awe and be reminded of the kind of God he serves.

His obedience: If ever this servant has any doubts about carrying out Elijah's instructions to keep checking the horizon, the high drama of this day will have silenced them. After everything Elijah did that day, what possible excuse could he have for not following this godly man's orders? Hence his obedience to keep going to the viewpoint to look for a cloud.

His patience: Closely related to his obedience is his patience. By the third or fourth trip to check out the weather conditions, the servant would have been entitled to tell Elijah, "Look, there's nothing there; this is pointless." But Elijah persists and the servant keeps going—seven times in all, which in Jewish thinking is the number that symbolizes completeness. His patience is rewarded.

~~~~~

We know nothing about this servant's life after this victory over Baal's prophets. We read in the next chapter that Elijah leaves town in a hurry, following the death threats of Jezebel. She wants revenge for the deaths of the prophets of Baal. The servant is now on his own, his master gone into hiding. Does he go back to his home, wherever that is, possibly to help out on the family farm? Does he attach himself to another prophet? Does he line up for unemployment benefits? Or maybe he too needs to flee and go into hiding, with Jezebel also wanting his life because of his association with Elijah.

We can only speculate. Of one thing we can be sure, however, that whatever his future looks like, it is cemented in an even deeper relationship with God because of that day on Mount Carmel.

17: Elisha — The Servant in Training

Read 1 Kings 19:15-21

Key Verse: *"So Elisha left him and went back. He took his yoke of oxen and slaughtered them. He burned the plowing equipment to cook the meat and gave it to the people, and they ate. Then he set out to follow Elijah and became his servant."* (Verse 21)

The great Elijah needs a successor and who better to fill that role than someone God selects? Which is exactly what happens when God gives Elijah explicit instructions to anoint his successor. Elisha both recognizes and accepts the call, symbolized in verse 19 by Elijah placing his cloak — a symbol of his own prophetic role — on his new apprentice. Elisha thus commits to becoming "the disciple and attendant of a wild, wandering and persecuted prophet," as the *Expositor's Bible* puts it.[38]

Elisha then asks Elijah for permission to say goodbye to his parents, which is granted. Next, he dramatically breaks from his current responsibilities in what is clearly a wealthy family and stops plowing in the field, slaughters the oxen he was using, and holds a feast to symbolize this significant transition in his life.

What happens next isn't entirely clear, other than that Elisha "set out to follow Elijah and became his servant." Other translations have "served him," "became his helper," and "ministered to him," all conveying a commitment to following wholeheartedly a man different from him in several important ways. Elijah spends much of his time in the countryside, living in caves in the desert; Elisha is mostly a city boy. Also, Elijah comes from modest means, possibly from a family of shepherds, according to the *Harper's Bible Dictionary*. Elisha's family is most likely wealthy (judging from the number of oxen used in plowing).

Various commentators stress the importance of Elisha's subsequent ministry, both at the personal level and in political affairs. Undoubtedly, Elisha is a worthy successor to his master. He must have been an astute learner, as an apprentice to Israel's legendary spiritual leader.

Why was that? One reason was that the senior prophet chose his protégé well. We don't know what dealings they had had before, but Elijah clearly saw potential in this man, potential that God affirmed, as we read in verse 16. He knew better than anyone the need for Israel to have a man of

---

[38] https://ccel.org/ccel/farrar/expositor1kings/expositor1kings.vi.xi.html. Accessed April 16, 2024.

deep faith to succeed him as its premier prophetic voice. The qualities he had lived out now needed to be cultivated in his successor.

Then, as we have seen, Elisha for his part acknowledges the call to this ministry by burning his bridges, so to speak, to mark a complete break with his current life. There is no turning back for Elisha, who foreshadow Jesus' words, "No one who puts a hand to the plow and looks back is fit for service in the kingdom of God." (Lk. 9:62) To remove any possible temptation to put his hand to his plow and turn back, he burns it. He kills his oxen and cooks the meat on the burning plow as he hosts a farewell feast.

Matthew Henry says of Elisha's apprenticeship that "It is of great advantage to young ministers to spend some time under the direction of those that are aged and experienced, whose years teach wisdom... Those that would be fit to teach must have time to learn; and those that hope hereafter to rise and rule must be willing at first to stoop and serve."[39] That willingness to "stoop and serve" is required of every servant. How much more important was it for Elisha to embrace the humility of learning and the faithfulness of serving that over time made him the worthy successor that his mentor and role model had hoped for.

---

[39] Matthew Henry: *One-Volume Commentary on the Bible*, 392.

18: Elisha's Servant — The Unseeing Servant

Read 2 Kings 6:15-17

Key Verse: *"And Elisha prayed, 'Open his eyes, LORD, so that he may see.' Then the LORD opened the servant's eyes, and he looked and saw the hills full of horses and chariots of fire all around Elisha." (Verse 17)*

What was going on with Elisha?[40] His capacity for seeing a more complete reality far outstripped that of his servant. We can only marvel at the depth of a faith and spirituality that enabled him to see things that almost all believers cannot. Even those of us who speak most fervently of our "Christian worldview" must concede that we do not see with Elisha's supra-human spiritual clarity. To be honest, we would seek psychiatric help for a loved one facing a life crisis, as Elisha did, who spoke of seeing invisible forces of help, whether these were the police, the military or a high-powered legal team.

But Scripture provides ample evidence that there *are* visible spiritual realities that are normally beyond our grasp. Dallas Willard said of this passage, "God enabled the young man to see the powers of his realm that totally interpenetrated and upheld all the normal, visible reality around him…"[41]

We struggle to find a rational explanation of how this surreal event could have occurred. Given the advances in post-Newtonian physics during the past century, the most brilliant minds from Albert Einstein onwards have left us with new and profound mysteries of how our universe works. A review of Philip Ball's book, *Invisible: The Dangerous Allure of the Unseen*, notes that there is much we cannot see because of our physical limitations. One example we can easily understand was the sneering opposition that Joseph Lister faced in trying to persuade people that invisible disease carriers existed. "'Where are these little beasts?' one physician wrote. 'Show them to us and we shall believe them.'"[42] At the other extreme of invisibility, Ball also examines the possibility of "alternate universes separated from ours by extra dimensions beyond the three spatial dimensions in which we are confined."[43]

---

[40] This Profile is adapted from Gordon S. Jackson, *Be Thou My Vision: Light, Sight, and the Christian Faith.*
[41] Dallas Willard: *Hearing God*, 79.
[42] http://www.dynamicscience.com.au/tester/solutions1/war/medicine/lister.htm. Accessed Sept. 4, 2023.
[43] *The Economist*, Aug. 19, 2014.

In the spiritual realm too, says John Chryssavgis, "There is always much more happening than that which is visible."[44] Quite possibly Elisha had been gifted with seeing a spiritual "fourth dimension" that enabled his ordinary vision to see things that, for the rest of us, apparently do not exist. But there are too many examples of the visually related supernatural in Scripture for us to dismiss out of hand the possibility of phenomena that could be explained only by the existence of an "alternate universe," or perhaps a "parallel" or "supplementary" one. Such a reality would help us to understand how a resurrected Jesus could appear through locked doors (Jn. 20:19) and how an angel could appear in Peter's prison cell and mysteriously remove his shackles and open barred doors. (Acts 12:6-10)

We are left with an unmistakable two-fold lesson from the story of Elisha and his servant: There are things in God's Kingdom that we are incapable of seeing, and God's mysterious power is always at hand. As *The Interpreter's Bible* notes regarding this episode, "[I]n every hour of peril and of apparent defeat the soul that trusts God is surrounded--if he has but eyes to see it--with divine spiritual agencies equal to any emergency."[45]

Elisha's servant was therefore able to set aside his fear, by overcoming his limits on sight.

~~~~~

We are almost certainly unlike either Elisha, with his profound spirituality, or Balaam, who played fast and loose with the living God and encountered what we see as the impossibility of a talking donkey. (Num. 22:28) So where does that leave us? For one thing, we must grasp as our starting point the reality of the psalmist's promise: "The angel of the Lord is on guard round those who fear him, and he rescues them." (Ps. 34:7) We are never out of the reach of God's care and concern.

We need to accept that we, like Elisha's servant, can never see the full picture of what God is up to around us as we serve Him. Our physical vision is limited in all kinds of ways. Similarly, we are each spiritually unique individuals, who see the spiritual realm differently. Our capacity to see God's world and His purposes being worked out around us varies widely. We range from those rare individuals who, with God's help, are able to have Elisha-like vision, to those who have voluntarily and willfully chosen spiritual blindness. Jesus has harsh words for these "blind guides," all the more so if they presume to take on leadership roles when they themselves cannot see: "If the blind lead the blind, both will fall into a pit." (Mt. 15:14)

But regardless of our place on that spectrum, each of us has the potential to change how we are and to improve our spiritual vision. We cannot snap our fingers and demand of God the equivalent of spiritual night goggles that He in the end gave Elisha's servant. But we can take steps that

---

[44] John Chryssavgis: *Light Through Darkness: The Orthodox Tradition*, 15.
[45] *The Interpreter's Bible*, vol. 3, 217.

will help us slowly improve our vision. If we are to change, so that we can better see the things of God around us as *they* are, the responsibility is on us; we cannot demand of God that He hand us those goggles to see things that are beyond our current range of spiritual perception.

Spiritually, Christians can be utterly confident in their belief that God's presence is with us in invisible and unknown ways. Moreover, that presence is by definition *good*. What we cannot see at present, as well as what lies ahead in our Christian journey, is unimaginably good. As Paul writes to the Ephesians, "Now to him who is able to do immeasurably more than all we ask or imagine, according to his power that is at work within us…" (Eph. 3:20) Or, as Ben Patterson put it, "God is up to something so big, so unimaginably good that your mind cannot contain it… What we see God doing is never as good as what we don't see."[46]

~~~~~

"O Lord God, in whom we live, and move, and have our being, open our eyes that we may behold Thy Fatherly presence ever about us." Bishop Brooke Westcott[47]

[46] Quotes in Gordon S. Jackson: *Quotes for the Journey, Wisdom for the Way*, 64.
[47] Quoted in http://assets.newscriptorium.com/collects-and-prayers/prayerscsl.htm Accessed April 16, 2024.

19: Gehazi — The Greedy Servant

Read 2 Kings 5

Key Verse: *"Gehazi, the servant of Elisha the man of God, said to himself, 'My master was too easy on Naaman, this Aramean, by not accepting from him what he brought. As surely as the LORD lives, I will run after him and get something from him.'" (Verse 20)*

We first meet Elisha's servant Gehazi in the previous chapter. But it is his perfidious conduct in Chapter 5 of our reading that demands our attention. The chapter begins with the story of Naaman, a Syrian general suffering from leprosy.[48]

The details of the cure don't concern us here. What does, however, is that Elisha refuses any of the lavish reward that Naaman is willing to offer for his healing. Elisha says in effect, "No payment is appropriate; the glory belongs to the God of Israel."

Having seen the wealth that Naaman brought to pay for his healing, a kind of oversized copayment, Gehazi figures he might as well get a cut. So even though Elisha makes it plain to Naaman that no payment is needed, Gehazi goes after the healed general and six things happen in unhappy sequence:

1. He decides to override his master's thinking and sets off after Naaman. Temptation has grabbed hold of him. The question is, will he resist it before acting upon it?
2. No. He catches up to Naaman and lies to him, fabricating a story that justifies why his master would like some of the goodies after all.
3. Naaman assigns two of his servants to carry the items, which include two pieces of silver; Gehazi had asked for only one. On getting home, Gehazi hides the items.
4. Then Elisha asks him where he's been, and he lies again, denying he's been gone.
5. Elisha confronts him regarding his deception, asking the poignant question, "Is this the time to take money or to accept clothes…?" (Verse 26) An act of great importance has occurred: A Gentile leader has experienced the power of Yahweh, the only true God. Naaman's healing has come by the grace of God, yet Gehazi has tainted this moment, perhaps leading Naaman to question what kind of God this

---

[48] See Profile 32 in this book, regarding the young Israelite girl who tells Naaman about Elisha, the Israelite who can cure him.

is whose seemingly generous prophet suddenly changes his mind and wants a material reward after all. No different, in other words, from the hypocrisy of some Christians today that continues to drive men and women away from the church.

6. Then follows the severe judgment that Elisha calls down on Gehazi, with him not only suddenly being smitten with leprosy but, we also read, "Gehazi went from Elisha's presence." Their relationship was shattered.

~~~~~

Maybe Gehazi's motives are honorable, at least in his own mind. As Elisha's senior servant, possibly he was in charge of money matters at the "company of prophets." Maybe two new members had arrived, as he had told Naaman. Money was always tight. It was all good and well serving a godly man like Elisha, but he didn't have to balance the books and make sure there was a suitable cash flow to keep the lights on. Or their equivalent.

A charitable interpretation some scholars have suggested is that he didn't want the money and clothes for himself; no, it *was* for the good of the order. A credible explanation? Almost certainly not. The six-step sequence described above portrays a man on a willful course of greed and deception.

It is not only that this once-faithful servant has fallen, it is a matter of how far he falls. Imagine being this close a servant to one of God's great men, Elisha, and forced "from his presence." E. M. Blaiklock says, "A bright and honorable future lay ahead of Gehazi. He was a natural successor of Elisha, as Elisha had been of Elijah. He wrecked all possibility of such usefulness by one act of greed."[49] Elisha's thinking may have prefigured what Friedrich Nietzsche said: "What upsets me is not that you lied to me, but that from now on I can no longer believe you."[50]

Of especial poignancy is how Gehazi wrapped his action in religious language. In verse 16, Elisha declines a gift from Naaman: "As surely as the LORD lives, whom I serve, I will not accept a thing." Then, four verses later, as Gehazi committs to his plan, he says: "As surely as the LORD lives, I will run after him and get something from him." He thinks that by using this religious formula he can sanitize the wrong he is about to do.

We read about Gehazi once more, in 2 Kings 8:1-6. He is summoned by King Jehoram to give an account of all the good things that his master, Elisha, has done. Perhaps, notwithstanding his leprosy, he has regained at least some of his status. We don't know if this followed any genuine repentance. We can only speculate on what has occurred with this erstwhile trusted, competent, and devoted servant, a man of great promise who succumbs to temptation in one moment of weakness. Sadly, his main contribution in the long run is to serve as a warning to us all.

---

49 E. M. Blaiklock: *Handbook of Bible People*, 299
50 Quoted in Gordon S. Jackson: *Never Scratch a Tiger with a Short Stick*, 144.

20: The Gibeonites — The Deceiving Servants

Read Joshua 9

<u>Key Verse</u>: *"We are your servants; make a treaty with us." (Verse 9)*

You get a phone call from your grandson, who is in jail in Missouri after being in a fight. He was attacked outside a nightclub, he says. His nose is broken, which explains why his voice sounds a bit odd, poor fellow. He urgently needs $2,400 in bail. Can you wire him the money?

Or there's that Nigerian prince (why is it always a *Nigerian* prince?) who has chosen you, yes *you*, to help move some of his millions out of the country — and he's offering you a 20 percent cut for being a conduit for the money.

Whether they're threatening calls from the IRS, the local courthouse telling you you've missed jury duty and need to pay a $200 fine to avoid immediate arrest, or... Oh, we all know these scams, and yet even the smartest among us fall for them. We do so because we're vulnerable in several ways. Our emotional chain gets yanked ("Billy, are you sure you're okay? Of course, I'll get you the money.") Or there's the stern, bullying voice on the line warning us of dire consequences if we don't immediately pay what we owe the IRS.

So we shouldn't be too harsh on Joshua and the children of Israel for falling for one of the earliest scams on record. The Gibeonites play on the Israelites' gullibility with their carefully crafted visual aids: moldy bread, worn clothes, old wineskins, and so on. The Israelites are riding high, following the victories over Jericho and Ai. As the *Africa Bible Commentary* notes, "Moments of victory and success are very dangerous times in our spiritual walk. It is often after successful exploits that we are most prone to imagine that we have everything under control. It is at such moments that we are prone to embark on projects without seeking God's will."[51]

When Joshua asks them where they are from, they instead refer to the fame of Israelites' great God, and all He has done in Egypt, and avoid answering the question.

So the Israelites are conned into making a treaty with the Gibeonites, even though they have come from only a few miles away and not the long distance they claimed. Which raises the question: What is prompting this charade? The short answer is they want to save their necks. As the Israelites continue to conquer bits of Canaan, the Gibeonites know that based on

---

[51] *Africa Bible Commentary*, 279.

Joshua's fighting strength they are likely to be high up on Joshua's "Canaanites-to-be-obliterated" list. The political realities of the Promised Land at this time meant constant turmoil and military activity.

The Israelites have been forbidden to make any treaties with the Canaanites. But even though they conclude this agreement unwittingly, there is another issue: As verse 14 indicates, they enter into it without consulting the Lord. This is atypical of Joshua.

When Joshua and his leaders discover the ruse three days later, they have two options. They can swallow their pride (and no doubt anger) and honor a solemn pledge they have made to protect these people. Or they can see the agreement as void, having been made under false pretenses. That's an idea we understand well in terms of contract law. If you've deceived someone about important aspects of a house you're selling, the buyer is well placed to sue you and void the contract. So why don't the Israelites toss out the agreement? Most likely because they fear it will bring dishonor to the name of Yahweh. As verse 18 says, "... the Israelites did not attack them, because the leaders of the assembly had sworn an oath to them by the LORD, the God of Israel." Knowing that their leadership has been duped, the people are angry at the need to honor this treaty. But as a compromise, Joshua assigns the Gibeonites the role of "woodcutters and water carriers," a conventional term for household servants. Essentially, they are reduced to slave status, a role they fill for generations.

Much later, when Saul is king, he violates Joshua's agreement by killing many of the Gibeonites. That is a wrong that David feels obliged to rectify, as we read in 2 Samuel 21:1: "During the reign of David, there was a famine for three successive years; so David sought the face of the LORD. The LORD said, 'It is on account of Saul and his blood-stained house; it is because he put the Gibeonites to death.'"

In a difficult to understand development, David hands over seven of Saul's descendants to the Gibeonites. They are then murdered and their deaths bring healing to the land. Such brutality reflects the long legacy of entering into an ill-advised treaty in the first place.

It is a painful and humiliating lesson that Joshua and his leaders learn. One hopes that they will be on higher alert if the next month a group of Nigerian princes come their way, seeking a treaty to protect them from the Amorites — in exchange for a fifty/fifty share of the great treasure they had buried in a secret location just outside Jericho.

21: The Innkeeper — The Beleaguered Servant

Read Luke 2:1-7

Key Verse: "[S]he gave birth to her firstborn, a son. She wrapped him in cloths and placed him in a manger, because there was no guest room available for them." (Verse 7)

Cast your mind back to all those Christmas pageants you've seen, and in some of which you may have participated as a child, dressed in an odd configuration of towels, pajamas or whatever else was supposed to make you look like an authentic participant in the marvelous nativity story.

Now, a question: How was the innkeeper in these pageants portrayed? Was he a sympathetic, kindly soul who wished he could help, but whose circumstances forced him to say, as Roland Bainton speculates, "My dears, I'm dreadfully sorry, but I just haven't any room"?[52]

Or did the pageant director tell the six-year-old filling the role to be as stern and dismissive as a child's voice would permit? Bainton cites an artistic portrayal of the innkeeper's refusal with him saying, "Get the hell out of here." Maybe the innkeeper mellowed enough to steer this exhausted couple to a stable, or maybe they found it on their own.

So, which kind of innkeeper would you have been? A sympathetic hosteller, committed to your role of serving the Palestinian public? But you didn't have room available and steered this couple to the best that you could offer them, your stable? And you didn't even think of charging them.

Or would you have been irritated by this peasant couple, who had possibly dragged you out of bed late at night? Maybe you were entitled to be irritated; possibly they were the fifth party to come knocking, desperately hoping for a place for the night. "Stupid travelers who don't plan ahead," you muttered. "Haven't they heard of hotels.com or Airbnb?"

Perhaps your temper was understandably frayed and your tone was harsher in your dismissal than you intended. Or maybe not. Maybe you were an unsympathetic jerk, uncaring about a woman on the verge of giving birth. That was *their* problem, not yours. Back to bed.

If you had been assigned the servant role of the innkeeper that night, what kind of person would you have been? How would you have liked to be portrayed 2,000 years later in nativity pageants around the world?

---

[52] These two alternatives are discussed in the artistic portrayals of the innkeeper, in Roland Bainton's *Behold the Christ: A Portrayal of Christ in Words and Pictures*, 38

22: James — The Enslaved Servant

Read James 1:1

Key Verse: *"James, a servant of God and of the Lord Jesus Christ, to the twelve tribes scattered among the nations: Greetings." (Verse 1)*

We could easily substitute Paul and Jude for this Profile. Each of them also begin letters to their fellow Christians by asserting their servant role. Here we read, "James, the servant of God, and of the Lord Jesus Christ ..." Paul begins Romans and Philippians the same way, describing himself as a servant of Jesus. Jude does the same in his epistle.

What do these writers whose epistles ended up in the New Testament mean by this statement? A clue emerges from the word each of them uses, *doulos*, the Greek word for slave. William Barclay's popular New Testament commentaries specialized in explaining for lay people important Greek words. Curiously, he translates *doulos* as "slave" in Romans, Philippians and James, but not in Jude, where he uses "servant."

That inconsistency is less important to us than the meaning of *doulos*. In his commentary on James, Barclay says it has at least four implications. "It implies *absolute obedience* ... *absolute humility* [and]... *absolute loyalty*." Fourth, he says, "at the back of it, this word implies a certain *pride*." He explains: "So far from being a title of dishonor it was the title by which the greatest ones of the Old Testament were known. Moses was the *doulos* of God...; so were Joshua and Caleb...; so were the great patriarchs, Abraham, Isaac and Jacob..." — among others, including the great prophets. "By taking this title," he continues, "James sets himself in the great succession of those who found their freedom and their peace and their glory in perfect submission to the will of God."[53]

The paradox of slave status for the Christian, as Barclay notes, is that it is in total submission to our heavenly Master that we find true and complete freedom, as our will is merged with God's. By accepting "slave status," Christians enter voluntary servitude, committing to a Master as "hyper-servants." Today, we rightly find the notion of slavery repugnant — from a human rights point of view, if nothing else. But Christians, who regard each person as someone made in the image of God, have added reason to reject slavery as something abominable to the Creator of all. Why, then, do we embrace the notion of slavery to characterize our role as God's servants? One reason is the absolute nature of the slave's position. There's no

---

[53] William Barclay: *The Daily Study Bible: The Letters of James and Peter*, 36.

negotiating our status with God; we are either fully, unreservedly, and absolutely His servants — or we are not. Christians forego whatever rights we think we have, recognizing that like slaves we *have* no rights. There's no unionizing among Jesus' followers for better working conditions or a better pension plan. Jesus' parable in Luke 17 is helpful in understanding our slave-like role:

> *Suppose one of you has a servant plowing or looking after the sheep. Will he say to the servant when he comes in from the field, "Come along now and sit down to eat"? Won't he rather say, "Prepare my supper, get yourself ready and wait on me while I eat and drink; after that you may eat and drink"? Will he thank the servant because he did what he was told to do? So you also, when you have done everything you were told to do, should say, "We are unworthy servants; we have only done our duty."*

On the one hand, this seems cold and abrupt; it seems the master is dismissive of the servant. We wonder if the master would benefit from attending a workshop on positive master-servant relations. Yet Jesus' point is this: We are never off duty as God's slaves; a slave is in effect a hyper-servant, one who has all the duties of a servant but none of the benefits that a servant might enjoy: pay, time off, possibly an employer-supplied uniform, and so on. Nor can we as slaves ever do too much for him. Even if we come in worn out from working in the field, there's still more to be done. As Meister Eckhart put it, "How can we ever be the sold short or the cheated, we who for every service have long ago been overpaid?"[54]

This readiness to commit themselves utterly and without reserve to Jesus and His demands of discipleship leads James, Paul, Jude and countless other heroes of the faith to proclaim their status as their Savior's slave. They would have it no other way.

---

[54] Quoted in Gordon S. Jackson: *Quotes for the Journey, Wisdom for the Way*, 73

23: John on Patmos — The Isolated Servant

Read Revelation 1:9-11

Key Verse: *"I, John, your brother and companion in the suffering and kingdom and patient endurance that are ours in Jesus, was on the island of Patmos …" (Verse 9)*

John was in exile on the island of Patmos when he received his apocalyptic Revelation, which now is the last book in the Bible. He was presumably banished there as part of a growing persecution of the young church. Although his freedom of movement was curtailed, his conditions were unlikely to have been as severe as if he were imprisoned. Unlike Paul, who was quite familiar with the inside of jails, John had it relatively easy. William Barclay says, "People so banished were not personally ill-treated and were not confined in prison on their island but were free to move within its narrow limits."[55]

Still, John was limited in what he could do in his condition, one that many of us might relate to. We may be experiencing what we'd be justified in regarding as our own kind of banishment. We may have put our career on hold to take care of an elderly parent, or a child with a serious chronic illness. Or we may have sustained severe injuries in an accident that have put us out of commission for a prolonged period. Alternatively, we may see ourselves more in a spiritual banishment. Our capacity to serve is stifled and we feel we're in limbo in our faith, stuck in a place where nothing especially bad is happening but we're not able to grow spiritually either.

However we might experience banishment, we can be assured that God has neither abandoned nor forgotten us. As Oswald Chambers says, "All your circumstances are in the hands of God; therefore never think it strange concerning the circumstances you are in."[56]

Then there is also the reality that God works even through those of us in some kind of banishment. It was while he was on Patmos, cut off from the young church in Jerusalem, that John received his stirring vision. It was from prison that Paul wrote several of the letters that now instruct and inspire Christians two millennia later.

Even though you may currently view yourself as being in a state of banishment, God never is. Nor has He forgotten to comfort, sustain and use those of His people who are.

---

[55] William Barclay: *The Daily Study Bible: Revelation*, vol. 1, 41.
[56] Oswald Chambers: *My Utmost for His Highest*, Nov. 7.

24: Malchus—The Injured Servant

Read John 18:1-10

<u>Key Verse</u>: *"Then Simon Peter, who had a sword, drew it and struck the high priest's servant, cutting off his right ear. (The servant's name was Malchus.)"* *(Verse 10)*

This was not how Malchus expected his evening to unfold.[57] As a servant of the High Priest, he was accustomed to working long hours on occasion. His duties were mostly routine, helping around the temple or taking care of things around the High Priest's home. So it was an irritation when the High Priest gave him this late night assignment of an undisclosed nature. When his wife kept asking why he was needed back at work so late, all he could do was tell her that he had no idea what the assignment was.

He was neither a security guard nor a soldier, however. So when he saw this detachment of Roman soldiers and their commander outside the High Priest's home, he was unsure why he was needed. The soldiers were drawn from the heightened Roman military contingent, always increased in Jerusalem during the potentially volatile time of Passover. Then he was further puzzled when he recognized, by the light of the numerous torches people were holding, a number of senior Jewish leaders. His puzzlement increased when he saw another figure, who was engaged in earnest but hushed conversation with the Jewish authorities: a man he recognized as one of the followers of the troublemaker rabbi whom all the Jewish leaders were talking about.

Then the Roman commander and one of the Jewish leaders had a brief exchange and the group set off. Still unsure of his role, which the High Priest had never spelled out to him, Malchus joined the procession, carrying his own torch of oil-lit rags.

The group was silent. Soon he realized the Jewish leaders and the Roman commander were heading to the Garden of Gethsemane, a short walk. When they reached the garden he saw a small group of men. He couldn't be sure who they were but he suspected one of them was the Rabbi Jesus, who had only this week caused such a disruption in the temple, overthrowing the money changers' tables and causing chaos for the worshippers. The follower of Jesus, whose name he later learned was Judas,

---

[57] This entry—and especially the conclusion—is fictitious, a speculation on what Malchus may have experienced. It is intended to spur your thinking on how his encounter with Jesus may have affected him.

went to the front of the group. He strode up to the one whom Malchus could now clearly see was Jesus. The man greeted Him with a kiss and said something he couldn't hear. Nor did he hear Jesus' response.

By now he was within a few yards of Jesus' group, when one of them came lunging toward him with a sword. Unarmed, Malchus raised his arms to protect himself, but too slowly. He felt a thud on his head as the sword struck, followed by a searing pain as the sword moved rapidly down onto his ear. To his horror, he saw what he instantly recognized as his ear lying on the ground. He could tell he was bleeding profusely from the side of his head.

Then the rabbi told His follower to put away his sword, which he did. "But too late for me," Malchus thought... Then, to his astonishment the rabbi bent down and picked up the ear, held it to the side of Malchus' head with one hand, and placed His other on the top of Malchus' head. He murmured something that Malchus couldn't hear, given the now boisterous and clamoring crowd, with the soldiers jostling around the rabbi and trying to get close enough to seize Him.

Malchus' concern, though, was his ear. Astonishingly, the pain was gone. The ear was in place, making him wonder if he had imagined the entire episode, which had lasted no more than a minute.

Then he stood bemused as the soldiers secured their hold on the rabbi and began taking Him away. By now, the few men with the rabbi, including the follower who had attacked him, had fled. The soldiers and others in the arresting party had no interest in them, it seemed. Also, with their mission accomplished, he saw no need to stay with the group. There hadn't been anything for him to do to this point, and there wasn't anything he needed to do now. He accompanied the group out of the garden then slipped away en route to his rooms at the back of the High Priest's home.

He turned the events of the past few minutes over and over in his mind, struggling to grasp the reality of his amazing healing—and to understand who this extraordinary rabbi was. What kind of man would not only put up no resistance but chastise His follower who tried to fight back? More amazing still, what kind of man had the power to restore a severed ear? Had he imagined this? Touching his ear repeatedly, as if he feared it could come loose at any moment, he could feel it was tender and still sticky with blood. The reality of his injury and subsequent healing were reinforced by his vivid recollection of seeing the ear on the ground.

No, he hadn't imagined this. Nor had he imagined the look in the rabbi's eyes as He brought about this miracle of healing. Jesus displayed an inexplicable serenity that was totally out of place in a man being arrested. He was quite unlike the person whom the chief priest and other leaders had discussed and plotted against this past week. Malchus had heard their assessments of how dangerous Jesus was as he waited on them during their meetings in his master's home. No, the rabbi was nothing like the man to whom they directed their fear and even hatred.

Arresting this man was unequivocally wrong. He knew that in his gut. But Malchus was a mere servant; he had no power or platform to speak out against this injustice. As he walked briskly in the increasingly cold night, he experienced a strange peace. He might be only a servant, but he could choose whom to serve. No matter what happened to this arrested rabbi, he concluded, he committed himself that night to serving Him instead.

25: Martha — The Over-Eager Servant

Read Luke 10:38-42

Key Verse: *"Martha was distracted by all the preparations that had to be made. She came to [Jesus] and asked, 'Lord, don't you care that my sister has left me to do the work by myself? Tell her to help me!'" (Verse 40)*

Someone once joked, "I have CDO; that's like Obsessive Compulsive Disorder but with the letters in the right order." Which raises the question, is Martha the Bible's premier sufferer of OCD? Is she so hung up on getting the house tidy, preparing the hors d'oeuvres, making sure the roast goes in at the right time, setting out a clean hand towel in the bathroom, checking her list once again to make sure she's not forgetting anything, that she loses sight of the big picture: the privilege of having Jesus in her home?

She's in a frenzy to do justice to the guest of honor, yet her sister sits on her butt, doing nothing to help. Her earlier pleas for help, or her several stink-eye glances in Mary's direction, have yielded no results. So she comes right out with it and implores Jesus. "Tell her to help me!" Jesus, she knows, will see the injustice of Martha having to do all the work; He's very good at calling out unfairness for what it is.

Instead, to her astonishment, Jesus issues a rebuke, to *her*! He tells her to cool it with her serving obsession. He says, "Martha, Martha, ... you are worried and upset about many things, but few things are needed — or indeed only one. Mary has chosen what is better, and it will not be taken away from her." (Lk. 10:41-42) You are focusing too much on the serving and too little on what's really important: attending to Me and what I have to say, as your sister is doing.

The Greek wording says Martha is distracted by much serving, using the word *diakonian*, from which we get "deacon." The word is presented positively elsewhere in the New Testament, so there was nothing wrong per se with her serving. The problem lay elsewhere, as Thomas Green, writing in *Darkness in the Marketplace*, explains. He draws a distinction

> between "working for God" and "doing God's work." At first sight, the two phrases appear equivalent but there is a crucial difference. Simply stated, the first is doing what we think God wants of us, giving him what we want to give him — what we think he needs and desires of us. Alternatively, "we can ask him what he would like and do whatever he wishes — do his work..."[58]

---

[58] Thomas Green: *Darkness in the Marketplace*, 48.

Green then offers the analogy of someone having a birthday and we give the person what we think the person would like rather than what they would actually like. Green says he likes blue cheese, which some people dislike intensely. But, he says, if you really wanted to please him, you'd give him blue cheese for his birthday — even if you find it repugnant. We may resist giving God the equivalent of blue cheese, because it repels us. Green continues:

> But it is the only way of being sure to please him. If, instead, we choose the gift ourselves — if we decide what we want to give him and what we think he really needs and should want — he will surely be grateful for and pleased by the love symbolized by our gift. But it may not be what he really wants and can really use.

Jesus undoubtedly sees Martha's devotion and service for what it is and appreciates her love for Him. She is "working for Him," giving Him what she thinks would please Him. To her surprise, though, Jesus calls her to reexamine her priorities. He's not nearly as interested in the hors d'oeuvres or whether the roast will be ready according to Martha's timetable. He is offering something more, something that Mary has intuitively grasped.

Jesus seeks to steer Martha away from two possible dangers. The first is that her priorities are out of whack. Always, her and our priority should be listening to Jesus. Mary seats herself at His feet, to attend to His teaching, doing the "one thing" that Jesus says is needed. *The New Jerome Commentary* says of these verses, "The lesson is not that one should prepare a casserole rather than a seven-course meal. One thing undergirds all following of Jesus: listening to his word, and that is the best part."[59]

The second possible danger is to avoid "working for God" rather than "doing God's work." Green points out that the second emphasis requires the hard work of discernment, to discover God's priorities for our lives, thus putting our wills in sync with His.

Thomas à Kempis said of some overzealous monks, "They presumed to do more than it was God's will for them to do, and so they soon lost the gift of grace."[60] Martha no doubt would have felt at home with this group, thus placing herself in danger of losing the gift of grace as she wore herself down with busyness.

William Barclay offers another insight into the different approaches of Mary and Martha toward their host. He notes that Jesus knew He had the cross before Him and all He wanted was the quiet in the home of good friends, a respite from the intensity of His ministry and the ordeal that lay ahead. Barclay says Jesus "had turned aside to Bethany to find an oasis of

---

[59] *The New Jerome Commentary,* 702.
[60] Thomas à Kempis: *The Imitation of Christ,* translation by Betty I, Knott, 122

calm away from the demanding crowds if only for an hour or two; and that is what Mary gave Him and what Martha, in her kindness, did her best to destroy."[61]

Imagine for example that you're in a restaurant, having a simple meal while you work on a vexing problem. You've escaped the office to concentrate on the issue before you. Cassie, the server whom we met in the Introduction, is on duty. Having taken care of your initial order, she keeps coming back asking if "everything is all right," topping up your coffee whether you want it or not and being far more irritating than helpful. She's giving you what she thinks is excellent attention, when all you want is to be left alone to work on your problem. At times like this you wish for a Mary rather than a Martha. If there's such a concept as "over-serving," Cassie is embodying it today.

Sometimes we see the Marthas in our church or Sunday School, or in some other ministry, shaming us with their examples of zealous service for the Lord. "What a saint she is," we may say to ourselves, "working so hard for God." Then we recall Green's distinction and we wonder if Jesus would take our saintly friend aside and say, "Martha, Martha…"

---

[61] William Barclay: *The Daily Study Bible: Luke*, 142.

26: Onesimus — The Useful Servant

Read Philemon

Key Verses: *"Perhaps the reason he was separated from you for a little while was that you might have him back forever — no longer as a slave, but better than a slave, as a dear brother." (Verses 16-17)*

Admittedly, calling Onesimus a servant is a stretch. He certainly isn't one by choice; he is a slave, and a runaway one at that, as Paul tells us in his remarkable epistle to Philemon. This letter is remarkable because it is unlike any other book in the New Testament: it is a personal letter written to Philemon, a man in Collossae who is Onesimus' owner. Onesimus had fled the city and gone to Rome (most likely, although there's some speculation Paul may have been imprisoned in Ephesus at this time). It is unclear if Onesimus stole anything from his owner, but verse 18 implies that he did, as Paul tells Philemon in essence, "Whatever he might have taken from you, put it on my account."

Since arriving in Rome (we'll assume that's where Paul is), Onesimus has not only encountered Paul, but the apostle has won him over to Christianity. He has subsequently become extremely useful to Paul in his captivity. Now, however, Paul is sending Onesimus back to his rightful owner, telling Philemon that the man who's returning is different from the one who fled: Onesimus is now a brother in Christ.

Paul makes an impassioned plea for Philemon to welcome back his slave, regardless of the wrongs he has done. A slave owner had absolute authority over what was seen as his property, including putting a slave to death if he wanted. Paul's letter, however, is so compellingly crafted that it is difficult to imagine that Philemon treats Onesimus harshly upon his return, let alone deciding to execute this new brother in Christ for absconding.

Some scholars think Paul is asking more of Philemon than merely accepting Onesimus back into his household. Rather, the argument is that Paul wants Philemon to free his slave and send him back, so he can continue to serve Paul in prison. In his letter, Paul plays with Onesimus' name, which in Greek means "useful" or "profitable." As the *Africa Bible Commentary* puts it, Paul is saying, "The one whose name means 'useful' was formerly useless to you [because he left you]. But now that he has been born again he will be useful. From now on his behavior will match his name."[62]

---

[62] *Africa Bible Commentary*, 1,488.

But what of Onesimus himself? Paul's letter says little about the man, other than his "usefulness" to him. We don't know how Onesimus came to be a slave. It seems highly likely, though, that Philemon frees him after getting Paul's letter. Matthew Henry, in his commentary, lists fourteen arguments Paul makes on Onesimus' behalf, championing his acceptance by Philemon. The persuasiveness of Paul's plea for Philemon to recognize his slave as a new man, a fellow Christian, is compelling enough by itself.

What happened to Onesimus in the long run? It is well known that later there was a bishop in Ephesus by that name. But scholars disagree over whether it was the same person, as this was a common name for slaves (and for former slaves as well). Setting aside the speculation over whether Philemon freed him, his possible return to Paul, or his ultimate role in the church, one tangible thing we can explore is his usefulness.

Another is his courage. He needn't have chosen to return to Philemon; he could have continued serving Paul and avoided the punishment that Philemon, under Roman law, is entitled to inflict on him, up to the point of death. Yet, persuaded by Paul and buoyed by the convictions of his new faith, he does the right thing and returns to make amends. Perhaps he continues serving Philemon for the rest of his life. Or perhaps, as we've indicated, Philemon frees him — which allows Onesimus to live out his faith as a voluntary servant, serving the local church, or perhaps returning to serve Paul. Or possibly even becoming the bishop of Ephesus.

Onesimus is mentioned in one other place in the New Testament. In Paul's letter to the Colossians he says that he's sending a certain Tychicus to the Colossian church, probably the person who's carrying the letter. "He is coming with Onesimus, our faithful and dear brother, who is one of you." (Col. 4:9) Quite apart from Paul's personal appeal to Philemon to accept Onesimus back as a Christian brother, here is his appeal to the Colossian believers to accept someone who is a "faithful and dear brother." Moreover, he *"is one of you."* Paul emphasizes Onesimus' equal standing in the Colossian fellowship that he is about to join, regardless of his status as a slave and despite the wrong he may have done to his owner.

Paul's championing of Onesimus' case reminds us that in our churches we should similarly be accepting of all fellow believers who seek to join us, regardless of their history or status.

Or it may be that we are like Onesimus, someone at risk of being rejected by a congregation that sees our past as too tainted for us to be accepted. This congregation may say in theory that they agree with George Stewart, who said that "The church after all is not a club of saints; it is a hospital for sinners."[63] Yet they apparently see us as the "wrong kind" of sinner, who, if we are accepted at all, will be into an isolation ward.

No, Paul insists; Onesimus — the slave — is to be welcomed

---

[63] Quoted in Gordon S. Jackson: *Quotes for the Journey, Wisdom for the Way*, 36.

wholeheartedly into the Colossian church. This servant of the Lord is now an equal, not a slave, an equal who belongs; for he is *one of you*.

27: Purah — The Overshadowed Servant

Read Judges 7

Key Verses: *"[The Lord said to Gideon] 'If you are afraid to attack, go down to the camp with your servant Purah and listen to what they are saying. Afterward, you will be encouraged to attack the camp.' So he and Purah his servant went down to the outposts of the camp." (Verses 10-11)*

Gideon's unprecedented victory over the Midianites is not likely to be taught at West Point, the US Army academy that prepares many of the nation's future military leaders. At least, not as standard operating procedure against the enemy. Yet this heroic tale of a previously timid Israelite and his against-all-odds victory is taught each year to millions of Sunday School children around the world. For good reason. It is a story of God working together with an ordinary (and initially fearful) man, overcoming his honest doubts, and inspiring him to embrace unorthodox military tactics to win the day.

Judges 7 describes the counter-intuitive way of selecting his fighting force, which leads him to whittle down the army from 32,000 men to 300. Gideon is rightly famous for this step but also for putting out fleeces as a primitive way of discerning the Lord's will. We say "primitive" because it contrasts with what God expects of Christians today. Blessed as we are by the presence of the Holy Spirit in our lives, tests like a fleece are inappropriate for the mature and thoughtful Christian. It is significant that after Pentecost, there are no indications of the disciples using lots or other fleece-like tests to discern God's will.

There's yet another sign that God uses to assure Gideon that victory lies ahead. In verse 9, God tells Gideon, "Get up, go down against the camp, because I am going to give it into your hands." That's where Purah enters the picture. He is described in various translations as Gideon's aide, bodyguard, armor bearer, servant and "boy." Possibly he was all of these. Understandably, Gideon completely overshadows Purah in this story. Sunday School children around the world learn about Gideon and his unorthodox victory. Few of these children could even identify Purah by name. No matter; modest though it is, Purah has a part to play, and it is worthy of our attention.

God tells Gideon to take Purah with him. At this point Purah would have been justified in thinking, "Are you kidding? This craziness has gone on long enough. First, you reduce your army from 32,000 men to 300. Now, you want to stick your head in the lion's mouth. Worse still, you want me to do the same." He could have said, "Count me out," and refused to go with Gideon.

But if Purah has any misgivings, Scripture doesn't tell us. Instead, he joins his master in what seems like an act of sheer recklessness. Yet his and Gideon's courage leads to the final word of assurance that Gideon needs to launch his attack. They get close enough to the Midianite camp to overhear the two enemy soldiers talking about the dream one of them had, a dream that they are doomed. As the soldier listening to the account of the dream says, "God has given the Midianites and the whole camp into his hands." (Verse 14).

This clinches it for Gideon, who launches the famous torches-trumpets-shout strategy, which drives the Midianites into chaos as they start attacking each other. Indeed, the only weapons used in this battle are the ones they turn on each other.

Gideon is rightly remembered as one of Israel's great judges. But he attains this victory only through God's help. He has human help too, of course: that of the 300 men who make the surprise attack possible, and the contribution of Purah.

Purah brings several qualities to this victory. We've already pointed out his courage. But also noteworthy is his loyalty. He swallows whatever fears he may have had out of loyalty to his master. However Gideon hears God's instruction to go to the enemy camp, he tells Purah what he has to do, and Purah has confidence enough in Gideon's leadership and trustworthiness to accept this is truly God's command. Purah clearly has sufficient faith in Yahweh to follow Gideon.

This battle is the sternest test yet of Gideon's leadership; he can very well be defeated and killed by the Midianites. The risks he faces are great. Yet Purah sticks by him, even to the point of being willing to go into the Midianite camp. Like any good servant, his loyalty is paramount.

It's significant too that God directs Gideon to take his servant. Why? Maybe it is for something as simple as companionship. Perhaps we have faced a challenge such as a potentially ominous doctor's visit, and we ask a friend or family member if he or she will come with us. The person may not need to do anything, other than provide a presence. If nothing else, Purah certainly provides that for Gideon.

E. M. Blaiklock says of Purah, "Add Purah to the list of worthy servants in the Bible."[64]

Worthy indeed.

---

[64] E. M. Blaiklock: *Handbook of Bible People*, 137

28: Rhoda — The Flustered Servant

Read Acts 12:12-14

<u>Key Verse</u>: *"Peter knocked at the outer entrance, and a servant named Rhoda came to answer the door." (Verse 13)*

Help me, Rhonda, the 1965 hit by The Beach Boys, could with a minor change easily be Peter's song at the door to the home of John Mark's mother. There he is, knocking on the door, saying, "Help me, Rhoda" — and being ignored.

Poor Rhoda. Maybe she is new at this servant role and hasn't finished watching all the training videos. Or maybe nothing in the tapes covered that you are supposed to open the door to people whose release from jail you've been praying for. Or most likely, as the passage suggests, she is so emotional she forgets the next step: Don't just listen to the knock and the voice: *open the door.*

Whatever the reason for her response, this is Rhoda's sole appearance in Scripture. This is her cameo role, and she blows it. Well, partly; she at least tells the others that Peter's at the door. Then she's told she's crazy, or that it must be Peter's angel. To her credit, she persists in telling them it is Peter who's knocking. But she still doesn't open the door. Eventually, Peter is admitted. As expected, the freed apostle takes center stage and Rhoda vanishes into obscurity, never to be mentioned again.

Before we snicker at her over-emotional reaction, let's note three things. The first, as we've already stated, is that she doesn't give up. She persists in trying to get the others' attention, with the goal of letting Peter in. She is clearly thrilled to hear his voice; that tells us that notwithstanding her servant role, her heart and commitment lies with this anxious group who have been praying for Peter's release.

Then there's the irony: Peter has experienced an angel-led escape from prison, in which the prison doors open on their own; he gets out of jail doors meant to keep him in. Then, flustered Rhoda unwittingly leaves him standing outside, not opening the door that should let him in. Peter may wonder, "Where's that door-opening angel now that I need him?"

Finally, there's a question: How would you or I respond in the face of a miracle? If I'd been told, for example, that my son was in a maximum security prison in Iran and a week later he showed up on the doorstep, how would I react? Flustered wouldn't begin to describe my response. Rhoda wouldn't be the only servant unsure how to respond to God's handiwork.

PART 4: THE UNIDENTIFIED SERVANTS

29: Abraham's Two Servants — The Oblivious Servants

Read Genesis 22:1-19

<u>Key Verse</u>: *"He said to his servants, 'Stay here with the donkey while I and the boy go over there. We will worship and then we will come back to you.'" (Verse 5)*

This is the account of God commanding Abraham to sacrifice his long-awaited son, Isaac. Yet Isaac was to be the vehicle for fulfilling God's promise of making Abraham the father of a great nation. The story is packed with drama, profound theological issues, and a miraculous conclusion. But our focus will instead be on the two unidentified servants who accompany father and son on this extraordinary journey, up to a point.

Maybe one of them was Eliezer, Abraham's senior and no doubt most trusted servant, as we saw in Profile 15. The text gives no indication who these two people were; they were presumably men but beyond that we know nothing about them.

Well, not quite. We can infer several things from the story. The first is that they were trustworthy. Abraham had asked these two people to accompany him on what could have been a cataclysmic trip, leading to the death of Isaac. Would they have had to help him bring Isaac's body home, on the donkey? Or would Abraham have left Isaac's body on the altar he made in God's honor? Abraham was preparing a burnt offering. Did that mean he might have left a charred body at the mercy of scavenging birds or other creatures? Or would he have tried to bring back what he could of Isaac's remains, and entrust the servants with whatever account he would give them of how Isaac had died? All these questions, then, speak to the fact that Abraham believed he could rely on the discretion of these two men.

The second quality these servants displayed was their obedience. We don't know how long the episode of Abraham's and Isaac's worship took. However long it took, these men waited with the donkey, as Abraham had told them. Did they suspect that their master was about to commit an act of child sacrifice? If so, they apparently kept this to themselves. Were they tempted to sneak up on their master and see if that was what Abraham was up to? No, they stayed at their post, oblivious to the drama that was unfolding a short distance away.

Nor do we know if these were pious men, who as members of Abraham's household had acquired the same kind of faith that we saw characterized Eliezer. If they were, they didn't suggest to Abraham that they'd like to join in the worship. Presumably they saw that as a private act to be conducted by father and son, and they kept their distance.

So they waited, totally unaware that they were within walking distance of an extraordinary event. Abraham's faith was being tested as never before, as Isaac increasingly realized *he* was the intended sacrifice. Then this private family drama culminated in God providing a substitutionary sacrifice, the ram caught in a thicket.

The two servants knew none of this. They quietly did their duty, perhaps taking turns napping as they kept an eye on the donkey. They spent their time chatting, perhaps about the cute new maid who had joined Abraham's sizable entourage. Or they were grumbling about their insolent teenage children, who nowadays showed no respect for their elders.

So it is with Christians today. We know virtually nothing of God's activities in our world. Like Abraham's servants, we've been given a task. Like those two men, we (usually) carry it out with diligence and faithfulness. But much is going on behind the scenes, with God directing a play in which we have only the smallest roles. We are unaware of most of the other actors and the parts they play. And that is perfectly fine. God neither needs nor wants us to know the entire script, or who is within walking distance but out of sight, living out his or her assigned role that is crucial for God's purposes.

We're waiting, looking after a donkey; that's all He's asked us to do and we're serving Him well as we do so. As the poet John Milton put it in a poem about his blindness and how it fit in with his faith in God, "They also serve who stand and wait."[65]

---

[65] Quoted in Gordon S. Jackson: *Quotes for the Journey, Wisdom for the Way,* 150.

30: The Bridegroom's Servants — The Gobsmacked Servants

Read John 2:1-11

Key Verse: *"…the servants who had drawn the water knew." (Verse 9)*

The servants witnessing Jesus' miracle of turning water into wine can best be described by that wonderful word in British English, *gobsmacked*, meaning "astounded," "speechless," or "overawed."

In John's gospel, Jesus' miracle is the first of the seven signs that the apostle records "to reveal his glory." In this well-known story Jesus saves the bridal party from the embarrassment of having under-catered for such an important event. We could spend time analyzing the theological significance of this sign and its foreshadowing of the Lord's Supper, the nature of the miracle itself, or the dynamics between Mary and Jesus and why He is initially reluctant to intervene but does so anyway.

Instead, we will examine the role of the servants in this episode and what we can learn from them. They engage in three actions. First, they listen to Mary and her instruction to do whatever Jesus tells them. Second, they follow His instructions to fill the six jars with water. Third, they follow His subsequent instruction to draw out some of what they assume is still water and take it to the person in charge of the catering, variously described as the master of the banquet, head steward, head waiter, or the "person in charge." Only now, when he samples the wine, do they know a miracle has occurred. Until then, the servants must have been rolling their eyes and stealing knowing glances at each other regarding the instructions of these strangely authoritative guests. "Who *is* this guy, and who is His mother, anyway," they might have asked, "bossing us around telling us to listen to Him?"

When the master of the banquet proclaims the wine to be excellent, the servants grasp what has happened before their eyes. At least, they grasp the fact that something inexplicable has happened. Was this Jesus of Nazareth some early version of the illusionist David Copperfield, who had fooled everyone with a brilliant trick? How did He *do* this? Did He switch the jars with some others when they were distracted? If they had been to the Greater Galilee School of Magic, they could have come up with other possible explanations.

Maybe there are sinister forces at work here. Has this Jesus fellow some kind of demonic powers, which in the Middle Ages might have got Him burned at the stake? But no, there is no scent of evil at work here. The wine is good, very good. Also, the action is worthy, saving a young couple from humiliation on the most important day of their lives. Then there is something strange, something inexplicably good about this man. There is a certain wholesomeness and an authority that help them understand why His mother told them to listen to Him. Here is a man who knows what He is doing. They are used to taking orders from all kinds of people. But this man's way of giving orders feels different; a certain magnetism marks everything He says and does.

Quite apart from witnessing the miracle itself, the servants know this encounter with Jesus will leave them forever changed. They can't understand what He has done, or how. But everything else at this wedding now feels irrelevant as they mull in their minds not only *what* they have witnessed, but *who* they have met.

Now, two millennia later, we are in danger of losing the sense of wonder that these servants experienced. We are so familiar with the stories of Jesus' miracles that it is difficult to relate to how these servants in Cana must have reacted. But they who had drawn the water knew; they *knew*. Those of us who have met Jesus should likewise say, "We know; we *know*." We too should stand gobsmacked.

31: The Centurion's Servant — The Needy Servant

Read Matthew 8:5-13

<u>Key Verse</u>: *"And his servant was healed at that moment."* (Verse 13)

One might question why the centurion's servant in this remarkable story of healing even merits a place in this book. One commentary after another on this passage discusses the amazing faith of the centurion who approaches Jesus, and understandably so. His servant is ill: "paralyzed and racked with pain," as the *Revised English Bible* puts it. He comes to Jesus for help, exuding a humility and depth of faith that astonishes Jesus.

How so? This healing miracle comes right after Jesus cures a man with leprosy. So, there's no question about this rabbi's ability to heal. But three things are different here, which might have given the centurion reason to doubt. One is that the leper was a Jew. We know that from Jesus' instruction that the now-healed leper should show himself to the priest, as Mosaic law prescribed. However, the centurion is a Gentile; perhaps the servant is too. Would healing be available to non-Jews?

Another is that the leper was there in person. The centurion is asking for something even more demanding of Jesus: that He do a long-distance, *in absentia*, healing.

A third reality that might have led the centurion to doubt is that he is asking for healing on behalf of someone else. Might the healer respond by saying, "I'll be glad to help but I need to see the patient in person. Can you bring him by tomorrow? I have healing hours between nine and noon."

Yet none of these realities deter him and so he asks for help. Jesus offers to come and heal him. (Note by the way the supreme confidence in Jesus' words. He doesn't say, "I'll see what I can do." No healing is beyond His ability.) The centurion says that's not necessary; Jesus need only give the word, and the servant will be healed. Jesus commends the centurion's faith, saying He has encountered nothing like it in Israel.

Jesus then speaks about God's Kingdom reaching even the Gentiles, like the centurion. The episode concludes with Jesus assuring the centurion that the servant is healed. We read in verse 13 that this is indeed what occurred.

We can only imagine how the conversation went upon the centurion's return home, how he must have described to his entire household the awe that this young rabbi instilled in him. And how, in some way, the centurion, the servant, and everyone else in the story were now drawn into this new order of things.

Until this point in the story, the servant has been mentioned only once, when the centurion announces the illness. Now the servant returns to the stage, again as a passive figure in the story. He does nothing to merit his healing. He has no speaking parts in this drama of long-distance healing. He probably doesn't even know that his master is intervening on his behalf. Yet that is exactly the lesson to be drawn from his situation. For without Jesus' intervention, we are like that servant. As Jesus says in the next chapter of this gospel, "It is not the healthy who need a doctor, but the sick… I have not come to call the righteous, but sinners." (Mt. 9:12-13)

We too are lying paralyzed, unable to help ourselves, in need of a miraculous intervention if we are to be restored to spiritual health. Fortunately, we don't need a centurion to let Jesus know of our condition; He already does. Just as the sick servant needed someone to plead his cause, so we too have an advocate — only ours is far superior. Even when we don't know what we need or how to pray for ourselves, the Holy Spirit is at work on our behalf: "[T]he Spirit helps us in our weakness. We do not know what we ought to pray for, but the Spirit himself intercedes for us through wordless groans." (Rom. 8:26)

Whatever malady we have, Jesus will remove and, like the centurion's servant, we will once again be fit to serve and fill our proper role in God's Kingdom.[66]

So, yes, on second thoughts, this servant's story applies to our lives far more than we might have thought.

---

[66] This is not to imply that every prayer for physical healing will be answered as we would like. Rather, the point is that God will equip us for the role He has in mind for us — even if that entails a limit on our physical abilities.

32: The Israelite Maid — The Magnanimous Servant

2 Kings 5:1-3

<u>Key Verses</u>: *"Now bands of raiders from Aram had gone out and had taken captive a young girl from Israel, and she served Naaman's wife. She said to her mistress, 'If only my master would see the prophet who is in Samaria! He would cure him of his leprosy.'" (Verses 2-3)*

We've already read these verses, in the story of Gehazi (See Profile 19). But unlike that identified man, here we encounter another of those many unidentified servants in Scripture, in this case a magnanimous young girl who found her place in history because of her generous spirit. Captured by the Syrians in one of their raids on the Israelites, this young girl ended up as a maid to the wife of Naaman, one of the Syrian generals.

Naaman, in turn, found his place in history because of his grave misfortune: he had leprosy. As Matthew Henry says of his plight, "Naaman was as great as the world could make him, and yet ... the basest slave in Syria would not change skins with him."[67] One can only imagine the gloom that descended on Naaman's household upon discovering his condition, and the fear. Despite his high status that Matthew Henry refers to, every aspect of Naaman's life was now in jeopardy.

His story culminated in his miraculous healing, despite his pomposity and petulance in dealing with the prophet Elisha. But it is not his story, and the lessons it could teach us, that interest us here. Rather, let us turn to the overriding lesson to be learned from this young maid: magnanimity. This is the quality of having a great or generous mind or spirit. Whereas this young girl had every reason to resent her plight, having been snatched from her home and reduced to slavery, her strength of character enabled her to transcend the temptation to seek passive revenge on this Syrian family. Instead of quietly withholding the answer she believed would cure her master, she generously shared the solution. Elisha the prophet would cure him. Even though she was Naaman's slave, she sought the best for him. As John Goldingay puts it, "She could have been pardoned for thinking to herself, 'This Aramean general deserves this disorder and more for what he has done to us Israelites, and to me in particular,' but instead she speaks up and tell her mistress about the prophet who could remove it."[68]

---

[67] Matthew Henry: *One-Volume Commentary on the Bible*, 405.
[68] John Goldingay: *1 & 2 Kings for Everyone*, 124

Somehow, through God's grace, she also transcended the trauma of being snatched away from her home in an Israelite village. We can infer that despite her slave status, she must have been treated reasonably well in her new setting, perhaps over time developing even some affection for her mistress and perhaps Naaman as well. While we don't know her age, we can assume she was old enough to fill the servant role. That meant she was also old enough to have been grounded in the faith of her Israelite family, and in Yahweh's power displayed in the prophet Elisha. When her captors took her from her village, the one thing she brought with her was her faith. She now readily shared this faith in this time of crisis. Craig Barnes said, "One of my seminary teachers once cautioned that any theology that does not hold up in the emergency rooms of life must be held suspect."[69]

She therefore earns her place in history, as "Once more a major role is played by a minor biblical character," *The Interpreter's Bible* says. "How little did she realize, this humble Hebrew girl, what her native piety — her only distinction — was to achieve. She did not hide her faith in God; she used it."[70] The commentator adds, "And let anyone today, however humble he may be, have faith in God and declare it to one in physical or moral need and he too may bring miracles to pass."

---

[69] Craig Barnes: *Yearning*, 23.
[70] *The Interpreter's Bible*, vol. 3, 210.

33: Jonathan's Armor Bearer—The Devoted Servant

Read 1 Samuel 13:16-14:14

Key Verses: *"One day Jonathan son of Saul said to his young armor bearer, 'Come, let's go over to the Philistine outpost on the other side.' But he did not tell his father... 'Do all that you have in mind,' his armor bearer said. 'Go ahead; I am with you heart and soul.'" (Chapter 14 verses 1 and 7)*

To do this Profile justice, you should read to the end of Chapter 14. The context is yet another round of military encounters between the Israelites and the Philistines. Jonathan is perhaps tired of his father's inaction. Saul is sitting under a pomegranate tree, waiting for we're not sure what.

So Jonathan decides to reconnoiter the Philistine positions, taking his armor bearer with him. But Jonathan's heroism and initiative lead to complications. They include what should be his death at his father's hand, which gets vetoed by Saul's fighting men. That's because of an ill-considered vow that Saul makes about killing anyone who has eaten, which Jonathan—unaware of the instruction—has unwittingly done. While the subsequent passage is packed with dramatic developments concerning Jonathan, we will concentrate only on the section that directly involves Jonathan's servant, his young armor bearer.

Jonathan finds an enemy detachment easily enough, and with remarkable trust in God devises a test to see if he should engage them. The armor bearer offers his wholehearted support: "I am with you heart and soul."

It is a remarkable statement, "I am with you heart and soul," says the *New International Version*. Other translations are:

- "I'm right here with you whatever you decide" (the *Holman Christian Standard Bible*);
- "I will match your resolve" (the *Catholic Bible*);
- "I am with you, as is your mind so is mine," (the *Revised Standard Version*), and
- *The Message* paraphrases it as "I'm with you all the way."

These various approaches all convey the wholehearted, unreserved support this young man offered his master. What can we infer from this brief response to Jonathan's suggestion that they check out the enemy position? First, we should note that these are the armor bearer's only words recorded in Scripture. Second, his statement exudes confidence in and loyalty to Jonathan. Approaching the enemy as they do requires remarkable courage, which the young armor bearer finds in two ways. One is the charismatic personality of Jonathan, who is inherently a more inspiring leader than his father. Especially in war time, we want to be able to follow into battle someone we trust. The other source of his courage is his shared faith in God, whose power Jonathan explicitly notes as they plan their attack. He says, "Perhaps the LORD will act in our behalf. Nothing can hinder the LORD from saving, whether by many or by few." (Verse 6)

A couple of verses later we read of Jonathan's test, saying that if the Philistines tell them to "come up," they will interpret that as God wanting them to engage—which is what happens. That's when the armor bearer joins Jonathan in attacking the Philistines, together killing about twenty of them. This throws the Philistine army into disarray and, coupled with an earthquake that terrifies them (the Philistines are convinced that Yahweh has intervened and their cause is lost), they flee the battlefield.

Regardless of our thinking about the brutality of war and the discomfort many Christians have about the God-approved killing of Canaanites, including women and children, our interest here is the servant role of this young man and the example he provides.

We too have a master whom we can fully trust, in every arena of life but especially when we're facing one of life's battles. This armor bearer may well have had no prior battle experience. But with Jonathan leading by example, he could enter the fray with confidence. So too with us; with Jesus leading the way, and with the Holy Spirit to guide us, we can be completely confident that our master is trustworthy and will secure for us a victory.

Jesus doesn't want half-hearted commitment. He says, "No one who puts a hand to the plow and looks back is fit for service in the kingdom of God." (Lk. 9:62) Instead, as we move forward with Him as our master, like Jonathan's young servant, we must say, "I'm with you all the way."

34: Nabal's Servant — The Diplomatic Servant

Read 1 Samuel 25

Key Verses: *"One of the servants told Abigail, Nabal's wife, 'David sent messengers from the wilderness to give our master his greetings, but he hurled insults at them. Yet these men were very good to us. They did not mistreat us, and the whole time we were out in the fields near them nothing was missing. Night and day they were a wall around us the whole time we were herding our sheep near them. Now think it over and see what you can do, because disaster is hanging over our master and his whole household. He is such a wicked man that no one can talk to him.'" (Verses 14-17)*

Curiously, the servant in this passage is seen by several commentators as so incidental to the narrative that he's completely ignored. Yet he is pivotal to the story. Yes, Nabal, David and Abigail are the stars, but surely this servant deserves an Oscar for best supporting actor. Without this servant's intervening role, David would have yielded to his anger and indignation and shortsightedly carried out a massacre of Nabal's household.

Re-read what this servant does, as he strategically approaches Abigail. He knows she has the common sense, decency and awareness of danger that are totally lacking in her boorish husband. Appealing to his impetuous master, he knows, would be a waste of time. He knows too that Nabal's insulting treatment of David's men will lead to the "disaster" that is "hanging over our master and his whole household." That includes him. He has suffered long enough under this unsavory character and put up with a lot. But he's not willing to sacrifice his life for someone for whom he feels no particular loyalty.

Abigail, by contrast, is open to reason. That is the strategy this servant pursues, perhaps on behalf of his fellow servants who are also appalled at how Nabal treated David's men. The servant gives a factual account to Abigail and appeals to her to think it over and then decide what to do. He concludes with the blunt statement that reminds Abigail, if any reminding is needed, that Nabal "is such a wicked man that no one can talk to him."

The servant is taking a great risk: one doesn't lightly tell one's mistress that her husband is a wicked and unapproachable man. She could have the servant severely punished for such an action. But the servant presumably knows what Abigail knows: that he's speaking an uncomfortable truth. He has assessed the situation accurately, judging by her response. She takes the servant's account seriously and takes immediate preemptive measures to forestall any attack by David.

The rest of the chapter tells of Abigail's shrewdness in getting David to back down from his plan to attack Nabal's household like a common bandit, a move that would have seriously jeopardized his reputation. Until now, David has been an outlaw in Saul's kingdom, but not a war lord or bandit. As the servant recounts to Abigail, David's men were protective of people like Nabal, and their flocks and servants. The expectation, in that culture, is that in return people would provide David's men with food as thanks for their protection. In his commentary, David Payne emphasizes that this arrangement wasn't a protection racket. He adds that "the people of Judah were his own folk, so the protection he offered them — from raiders like Amalekites and Philistines, or from occasional wild animals — was freely given in the hope of a generous response in terms of food, no cash."[71] On the contrary, Payne continues, "Demands with menaces would have been quite fatal to his cause, ... alienating the only people who might offer help."

David's impulsive decision to attack Nabal, with 400 armed men, is grounded in anger. He should have heeded the advice of a twentieth century Japanese diplomat who said, "Never get angry, except on purpose."[72] David hasn't thought through the implications of an attack on Nabal, to repay the man's insult. If the attack had gone ahead, there's no telling what that might have done to David's standing among the people who would one day accept him as their king. He may well have lost political support vital to the outworking of God's plan. Thanks to Abigail, a savvy and courageous woman, David abandons his plan. He avoids a disaster and as a bonus ends up marrying the woman who has prevented him from making a political blunder and an act of needless brutality.

In the long run, it is not only Abigail whom David should be thanking. He should also thank the unidentified servant who assessed the situation facing Nabal and his household, and acted like a United Nations peace emissary to secure Abigail's intervention.

Whether or not the servant deserves an Oscar for best supporting role, he should certainly be on the short list for a Nobel Peace Prize.

---

[71] David Payne: *1 & 2 Samuel*, 130.
[72] Quoted in Gordon S. Jackson: *Never Scratch a Tiger with a Short Stick*, 28.

35: Peter's Problem People — The Hostile Servants

Read Matthew 26: 69-75 and Mark 14:66-72

Key Verse: *"Then Peter remembered the word Jesus had spoken: 'Before the rooster crows, you will disown me three times.'"* *(Mt. 26:75)*

There are several differences in the denial stories in the four gospels. Mark's gospel, for example, which was written before Matthew's, says that it was the same servant who twice identified Peter as one of Jesus' disciples (verses 66-69). Matthew says Peter's first two denials were to separate servant girls: In verse 71 Matthew refers to *another* servant. Then, Luke (22:58) says the second denial was to a man; Matthew and Mark say it was a servant girl.

These differences in details, however, don't detract from the substance of the story, which would have been well known to the early church. In the heat of the moment, the man who had the courage to follow the arrested Jesus to the High Priest's home found his courage failing him and he denied his Lord repeatedly. The conflict in the details pales into irrelevancy compared with the impact these three denials had on Peter. He was devastated. No wonder the sound of a cock crowing led him to burst into tears as he recognized what he had done to his Lord and master.

He experienced what the poet Edwin Markham wrote, that "Defeat may serve as well as victory to shake the soul and let the glory out."[73] We could say much more about Peter's experience and Jesus' subsequent embrace and restoration of this man. But we need to turn our attention to the three servants who served as the catalyst for Peter's repeated denials. What are we to learn from them? For want of a better term, we can describe them as hostile servants. None of them were in Jesus' camp. However, even though they couldn't know the implications of what they were doing, they held Peter to account — and he failed the test they presented him.

Christians should hold each other to account, lest we let down or embarrass our Lord, our church, or ourselves, and bring dishonor to Christ's Kingdom. But sometimes no other Christians are around and the only people noticing our behavior are, like these three servants, serving another master.

At times, those questioning us or holding us to account may be other Christians, but perhaps with major differences in theology compared with

---

[73] Quoted in Gordon S. Jackson: *Never Scratch a Tiger with a Short Stick*, 70.

us. We may serve the same master but interpret His orders or expectations differently, for example on the nature of baptism or the Lord's supper.

Notice too that the people confronting Peter were *servants*. Would we be more forgiving of Peter if it were the High Priest himself or a centurion who accused him of being one of Jesus' followers? The servants had no authority, yet it was at their accusations that he trembled and uttered his denials with curses. One could understand Peter's fear of the unknown, as he had no way of predicting what would happen to Jesus and his instinct to save himself prevailed. Would any of us have done differently? Another take-away, then, is the power of the seemingly powerless — mere servants — to precipitate an event so significant that Peter's denial made it into each of the four gospels. Even though these servants couldn't know how important their role was in Peter's life, they were indispensable in shaking his soul and, ultimately, letting the glory out.

36: Saul's Servant — The Resourceful Servant

Read 1 Samuel 9

Key Verse: *"[T]he servant replied, 'Look, in this town there is a man of God; he is highly respected, and everything he says comes true. Let's go there now. Perhaps he will tell us what way to take.'" (Verse 6)*

Former British Prime Minister Margaret Thatcher said, "No one would remember the Good Samaritan if he'd only had good intentions; he had money as well."[74] To some extent, that applies to this final servant whom we'll discuss: the man who accompanies Saul in his quest for some missing donkeys.

1 Samuel 9 portrays Saul as rather hapless. His father instructs him to find the missing donkeys, valuable property in that day, serving as the trucks we use nowadays to move goods. We don't know how many donkeys were involved but the text says *"the donkeys,"* implying all of them, thus heightening the importance that they be found.

So off Saul goes on a donkey hunt, accompanied by his servant, yet another of the unidentified people who have their part to play in God's plan. In this case, the servant, referred to in some translations as a boy, brings a resourcefulness to the situation that proves indispensable. The search doesn't go well. They go through Ephraim, the territory around Shalisha, the district of Shaalim, the territory of Benjamin and finally the district of Zuph, without success. Three days go by.

By now, Saul is concerned that his father will have filed a missing persons report, they've been gone so long. At this point the servant shows his resourcefulness. No doubt he is as frustrated as Saul is at their lack of success. So he suggests they stop and ask for directions. He knows that in the town they're approaching, presumably Ramah, there lives a seer or prophet. We know him to be Samuel. It is noteworthy that Saul — Israel's future monarch — apparently has no knowledge of this man. The *New International Version* study notes say, "Saul's ignorance of Samuel is indicative of his character." He clearly isn't well informed or well connected politically, whereas even his servant knows of Samuel by reputation, although he doesn't know his name.

Nor, when Saul agrees to consult the seer, does Saul have any money. Again, it is the servant who is equipped. He has some cash handy, which etiquette requires they offer the prophet. Again, he shows his assertiveness.

---

[74] https://www.forbes.com/quotes/11410/. Accessed Sept. 5, 2023.

As the *Revised English Bible* has it, he tells his master, "Wait! I have here a quarter shekel of silver. I can give that to the man, to tell us the way."

Samuel is expecting Saul, as God has told him to expect Israel's first and future king. So upon meeting Saul and the servant, he assures them that the donkeys have been found and tells them to stop worrying. He then invites the newcomers to a feast that was scheduled for that night. We're unsure of the occasion; some writers think it may have been a wedding feast. Whatever the event, about thirty people were gathered, no doubt all of them puzzled by the late inclusion of these two strangers. Even more puzzling is Samuel's order to set the choicest piece of meat before Saul, an unexpected honor that Samuel doesn't explain.

An explanation, at least for Saul, comes the next morning. Samuel tells the servant to go on ahead and then anoints Saul as Israel's future king. Having played his part in bringing Samuel and Saul together, the servant knows his place and leaves these two men to conduct whatever business they have, business of great national importance. While he doesn't know what they have discussed, he gets to see Saul possessed by the Spirit on their way home. This event must have greatly impressed the servant, who may well put one and one together—if not then, perhaps later when Saul is installed as king.

For now, the servant has played his part. Yet what if he hadn't known about the prophet in Ramah? Or hadn't suggested they check in with him? Or didn't have a coin to pay the prophet and just decided they'd turn round and start heading home? God could certainly have found another way to bring Saul and Samuel together. The fact is, though, that God chose to work through this initiative-taking servant, who is in the right place at the right time. And with the right disposition: a readiness to serve with initiative and assertiveness.

PART 5: CONCLUSION

Conclusion: "I'll Be Your Server"

Read Galatians 1:10

Key Verse: *"Am I now trying to win the approval of human beings, or of God? Or am I trying to please people? If I were still trying to please people, I would not be a servant of Christ." (Verse 10)*

Let us return to our server Cassie, whom we met in the Introduction. She has had a good shift: pleasant customers, smooth cooperation with the kitchen, and a good haul in tips, which tonight totaled $87. Each of her customers, if we had the chance to ask them, would say Cassie served them well.

What about those of us who profess to serve Jesus as Lord? How well would He rate our service today? Or the past week or month? Let us look back at the thirty-five case studies and identify the main features that emerged from our exploration of a wide range of people, features Jesus would expect of us. Some of those we met, like Moses, Mary and Paul, provide models of servanthood, as does Jesus Himself.

Among the positive servant qualities we saw were courage, obedience, loyalty, patience and empathy, all rooted in a godly humility. We saw that what set Christian servanthood apart was a whole-hearted commitment to following Jesus' example and seeking God's will for our lives. In other words, Christians are driven in all aspects of their lives by a godly motivation. Good servants can work for a variety of worthy and noble motives; *Christian* servants seek to please their Lord.

What else? Some of these servants received an explicit call to service from God, such as Moses or Mary. Others responded to the circumstances in which they found themselves, like Saul's servant helping him to find the missing donkeys. Likewise, some of us will receive a call to a specific ministry or service, or already have. Others of us will live out our service in response to the circumstances we face. Either way, Paul's words to the Corinthians are pertinent: "Each person is given something to do that shows who God is." (1 Cor. 12:7, *The Message*) Commenting on this verse, F. W. Grosheide says of Christians that "everything one possesses or is allowed to use must be used in such a manner that it is to the glory of God and the well-being of one's fellow creatures."[75] Which is another way of saying we are to serve God and each other — and doing that requires an ongoing sensitivity to the leading of the Holy Spirit in our lives.

---

[75] F. W. Grosheide: *The First Epistle to the Corinthians*, 284

Regrettably, we also saw some negative examples of servanthood gone wrong. Characters like Doeg or Gehazi show us how *not* to engage in God-honoring service. For the most part, though, the Bible characters whom we met were people of positive action. Service by definition means *doing* something. Moses didn't sit around pondering what it would be like if the children of Israel were freed from slavery. He did something about it. Jonathan and his armor bearer took the battle to the enemy. Paul risked his life repeatedly in sharing the gospel with hostile audiences.

We love to read about the luminaries of the faith, like Paul. And David, Moses, Mary, Gideon. But we must never overlook the "little people" whom we met in Part 4, those who didn't even get their names in the biblical narrative. Most of us are more like them than anyone else. In a hundred years' time, few of us will be remembered or recorded in history books. Regardless of our contributions to humankind and to God's Kingdom, the fact is that relatively speaking, we will have lived ordinary lives. Few if any readers of this book will win an Oscar or Nobel Prize, or have a biography written about them. Few if any will become a Billy Graham or Mother Teresa or Martin Luther King Jr. Few if any will achieve great scientific breakthroughs or become a creative genius in the arts or in literary accomplishments. Yet the lives we have lived will count for plenty in God's eyes. Our quiet service will, like that of the unidentified servants of Scripture, shape and advance God's Kingdom in ways we cannot imagine.

~~~~~

Although not speaking from a Christian point of view, Bill Gates told a 2007 class of graduating high schoolers: "The final measure of your life won't be how well you live—but how well *others* live, because of you."[76] That sounds a lot like service, service on which followers of Jesus need to superimpose a godly purpose and a commitment to advancing God's Kingdom however He leads us. We do so by responding to Jesus' call to action as we aspire to serve our Lord and Master.

Cassie our server didn't do justice to her diners this evening by contemplating on their orders; she *acted*. So too must we. While there's unequivocally a need for meditation, contemplation and prayer in our spiritual lives, God expects us also to be people of action. As James wrote, "Be ye doers of the word, and not hearers only..." (Jas. 1:22, *King James Version*)

As we grow and mature in our faith, the quality of our Christian service should mature as well. This could emerge from a deepening understanding of how God guides us; from a greater understanding of our servant-master relationship with him; or perhaps some other way. But however it occurs, our more Christ-like servanthood should correspond

---

[76] https://www.seattletimes.com/seattle-news/bill-melinda-gates-speak-at-nieces-graduation/. Accessed Sept 5, 2023.

with John the Baptist's mandate: "He must become greater; I must become less." (Jn. 3:30)

John's comment is about us being on a trajectory of improved or heightened service for our Lord. Just as we'd expect Cassie to become a better server the more experience she gained waiting on diners, so too ought we to grow in our service of waiting on our Lord. But what if we suspect that's not happening? Either way, some adjusting is needed.

Lastly, we have a choice on how to engage in the Christian service that awaits us. We can do our duty with a grim determination, or with the joy that Jesus said we could find in Him and His service. He would undoubtedly prefer the latter. We would do well to emulate the view of the composer, Franz Joseph Haydn, who said, "Since God has given me a cheerful heart, he will forgive me for serving him cheerfully."[77]

So we stand each day before our Lord, needing to choose afresh to whom we will give our whole-hearted loyalty. Once again, let our response be, "I'll be Your server."

---

[77] https://www.azquotes.com/quote/1342018. Accessed Sept. 5, 2023.

Acknowledgements

The following friends read the initial manuscript of this book and I am much in their debt for their critiques and suggestions: Malcolm de Kock, Jeff Haschick, Dia Maurer, Lisa McLean and Hans-Pieter Schragg. Their feedback was immensely helpful in shaping the final product.

My actor son, Matthew, brought his uncanny proofing skills to bear on the manuscript, catching numerous typos.

I also need to thank Tamera Kraft, the Executive Editor at Mt Zion Ridge Press, for her enthusiastic support for this project, as well as Michelle Levigne, the Press' Editor in Chief for her rigorous editing of the manuscript. I am most grateful to each of them.

ABOUT THE AUTHOR

Gordon S. Jackson is a South African-born educator and author. He grew up in Cape Town, where he received his undergraduate education. He then completed an MA at Wheaton College in Illinois and worked as a reporter and editor for a newsmagazine in Johannesburg.

Returning to the United States, he then completed his doctorate in mass communication at Indiana University in 1983. He then began his teaching career at Whitworth University, a liberal arts institution in Spokane, WA. He retired in 2015 but has remained active as an author.

I'll Be Your Server is his twentieth book. In addition to two scholarly books, he has written three satirical novels, an anthology of satirical pieces about the church, and several other faith-related books.

He is married to another South African, who helps to keep his accent honest. He and his wife have two adult children and identical twin granddaughters, who have been officially certified as the cutest, brightest, and most engaging grandchildren in the continental USA.

THANK YOU!

Thank you for reading this book from Mt. Zion Ridge Press.

If you enjoyed the experience, learned something, gained a new perspective, or made new friends through story, could you do us a favor and write a review on Goodreads or wherever you bought the book?

Thanks! We and our authors appreciate it.

We invite you to visit our website, MtZionRidgePress.com, and explore other titles in fiction and non-fiction. We always have something coming up that's new and off the beaten path.

And please check out our podcast, **Books on the Ridge,** where we chat with our authors and give them a chance to share what was in their hearts while they wrote their book, as well as fun anecdotes and glimpses into their lives and experiences and the writing process. And we always discuss a very important topic: *Tea!*

You can listen to the podcast on our website or find it at most of the usual places where podcasts are available online. Please subscribe so you don't miss a single episode.

Thanks for reading. We hope to see you again soon.

www.ingramcontent.com/pod-product-compliance
Lightning Source LLC
Chambersburg PA
CBHW011223120626
46545CB00010B/3124